DAN SCHLOSSBERG

CB

CONTEMPORARY
BOOKS
CHICAGO · NEW YORK

Library of Congress Cataloging-in-Publication Data

Schlossberg, Dan, 1948–
    The baseball IQ challenge / Dan Schlossberg.
        p.   cm.
    ISBN 0-8092-4526-4
    1. Baseball—United States—Miscellanea.   I. Title.
GV867.3.S344   1988
796.357'0973—dc 19   88-30294
                                                  CIP

Published by Contemporary Books, Inc.
180 North Michigan Avenue, Chicago, Illinois 60601
Manufactured in the United States of America
Library of Congress Catalog Card Number: 88-30294
International Standard Book Number: 0-8092-4526-4

Published simultaneously in Canada by Beaverbooks, Ltd.
195 Allstate Parkway, Valleywood Business Park
Markham, Ontario L3R 4T8 Canada

This book is dedicated to the memory of my father, Dr. Ezra Schlossberg, who always knew all the answers—in baseball and in life.

• CONTENTS •

• INTRODUCTION •
ROUNDING THIRD . . .
AND TRYING TO SCORE

Scoring is everyone's mission in life—not only on the basepaths but also in both professional and personal relationships.

This book has a similar objective.

Some 700 questions, divided into 16 chapters, cover the entire spectrum of the game, from Hoboken to the Homerdome, and offer both casual and avid fans the chance to determine their Baseball IQ both by topic and overall knowledge. In each chapter, the familiar academic marking system determines your ranking as a student of the game.

Picking 700 questions that would best fit this format was hardly an easy task; baseball, perhaps because its season extends nearly nine months, generates questions the way Krakatoa spews lava. Even professionals play the trivia game; wherever writers gather, they invariably begin quizzing one another.

Had personal feelings prevailed, this book would have been overloaded with questions about the Milwaukee and Atlanta Braves. In 1957, when the

Dodgers and Giants decided to abandon the New York area, all my friends focused their loyalties on the only team in town, the Yankees. As a nonconformist, my objective was to find a better team, one that would enable me to do to them what Braniff used to tell travelers: "If you've got it, flaunt it."

The Braves, world champions of 1957, gave me that opportunity by winning a seven-game World Series against the Yankees. So what if it's been all downhill since? Three of my heroes from that team—Hank Aaron, Eddie Mathews, and Warren Spahn—have all become Hall of Famers.

I still can't believe they laughed at Passaic High School when I predicted 10 years before the fact that Aaron was going to break Babe Ruth's career homerun record. They're not laughing anymore; a Brave has beaten a Yankee.

Ruth, Aaron, and the other greats of the game appear frequently in baseball literature—especially in publications that were the primary sources for this book.

Major references included two of my previous books, *The Baseball Catalog* and *The Baseball Book of Why*, along with the publications of the Society for American Baseball Research (SABR); *The Sports Encyclopedia:Baseball* (St. Martin's Press) by David S. Neft and Richard M. Cohen; *The Sporting News Baseball Trivia Book*, coedited by Joe Hoppel and Craig Carter; *The All-Star Game* (*The Sporting News*) by Donald Honig; *The Series* (*The Sporting News*) by Joe Hoppel and Craig Carter; Joe Reichler's *Baseball Encyclopedia* and *Baseball Record Companion* (Macmillan); Ev Cope's *Rounding Third* newsletter; Bob Davids's annual *Baseball Briefs*; and the *Encyclopedia Americana Yearbooks* for 1987 and 1988.

Detailed baseball scrapbooks, kept daily during

the season, also helped in gathering the questions on the pages that follow. Sportscaster Kevin Barnes of Atlanta and memorabilia collector Bill Jacobowitz of Livingston, New Jersey, also deserve special thanks.

This book is designed to foster friendly competition among friends during rain delays, long winter nights, or lazy beach afternoons before night games. It is my hope that you enjoy reading it as much as I did writing it.

—Dan Schlossberg

• SCORING •

As you complete each chapter, add up your score according to the scoring chart. When you've finished the entire book, add up your scores from each chapter to determine your baseball IQ:

700	Whitey Herzog Award—ready to manage in the majors.
600-699	Billy Martin Award—excellent but not perfect; could be fired and rehired frequently.
500-599	Chuck Tanner Award—eternal optimist even in the face of disaster.
400-499	Don Zimmer Award—workmanlike knowledge of the game.
300-399	Frank Robinson Award—good but hardly Earl Weaver.
200-299	Cookie Lavagetto Award—only the Senators would hire you.
100-199	Joe Frazier Award—anyone could have managed those Mets.
Under 100	Back to the minors for more seasoning.

• 1 •
HITTERS

Baseball's mystique—the ingredient that makes it America's most popular sport—is best explained by the simple act of hitting the ball.

With one swing, a hitter can change the complexion of a game—or a season. But even the most successful hitters fail about seven times out of ten; Ty Cobb, the career leader in batting average, made an out 63.3 percent of the time he came up to the plate.

Teams win championships with a blend of timely hitting, good defense, and effective pitching. A shortage of any of these three ingredients usually precludes pennant contention.

Because hits mean runs, teams treasure batters who can get on base, whether by hitting, walking, or being hit by pitches. Good contact hitters are also valued. A strikeout gains nothing, but a ground ball or long fly may produce a run or move runners into scoring position.

Babe Ruth, known for exploits both on and off the field, was especially adept at producing large numbers of runs. In 1923 he reached base 54 percent of the time, scored 151 runs, and knocked in another 131. He had a .393 batting average, 41 home runs, and a major-league record 170 walks.

Ruth's single-season and career home-run marks later fell to Roger Maris and Hank Aaron, respectively, but many historians still regard Ruth as baseball's greatest hitter. A case can also be made for Rogers Hornsby, Ted Williams, Joe DiMaggio, Mickey Mantle, or Stan Musial, as well as Cobb or Aaron. Study this chapter and decide for yourself.

• SCORING •

How much do you know about hitting? Here's how to grade yourself:

95–110   Grade A. You've won the Babe Ruth Award.

85–94   Grade B. Not bad. Stan Musial never won a home-run crown either.

75–84   Grade C. Passable. Harmon Killebrew couldn't hit for average.

65–74   Grade D. Back to the minors for more seasoning.

Under 65   Grade F. It's unconditional release time.

• QUESTIONS •

1. Whose consecutive-games-played streak did Lou Gehrig break?

2. What two players hit the most home runs during the time they were together as teammates?

3. What brother tandem hit the most combined career home runs?

4. Who is the only National Leaguer to hit two grand slams in a game?

5. Name one of the three active players who went directly from college to the majors.

6. Who led or tied for the NL home-run crown seven straight years?

7. How many intentional walks did Roger Maris receive when he hit 61 home runs in 1961?

8. Name four positions played by Harmon Kille-brew in the majors.

Harmon Killebrew became a star only after he abandoned his original position.

9. Name one of the two men who hit four home runs in a game his team lost.

10. Who hit four home runs and a double, for a record 18 total bases, in one game?

11. Who holds the record for lifetime pinch hits?

12. Name one of the two Braves sidelined for a season by tuberculosis.

13. What two players each stole 70 bases and had 70 RBI in one season?

14. What two active players each hit four home runs in a game?

15. Name the only player with 40 homers and 40 steals in a season.

16. What was Pete Rose's original position?

17. For what team did Dave Johnson once hit 43 homers in a season?

18. What trio of teammates each hit 40 home runs in 1973?

Davey Johnson, who later became manager of the Mets, became a surprise slugger following an interleague trade.

19. What quartet of teammates each hit 30 home runs in 1977?

20. What three brothers batted in the same inning for the same team?

21. Name at least three active players whose dads played in the majors.

22. What four Braves hit consecutive homers in a 1961 game?

23. What four Indians hit consecutive homers in a 1963 game?

24. Name two players who played all nine positions in a game.

25. Who is the only player in this century to go 7 for 7 in a nine-inning game?

26. Who was the last player to hit 50 home runs in a season?

27. Who was the first black player in the American League?

28. Who was the only player to have a 30-homer, 30-steal season more than twice?

29. Name the only player to have 40-homer seasons in both leagues.

30. Who was baseball's oldest home-run king?

31. Who was the only major-league player killed by a pitched ball?

32. What third baseman hit the most homers in a season?

33. Who holds the single-season National League home-run record?

34. Name three players with at least 600 career homers.

35. Who was the first designated hitter?

36. What nonpitcher played in more than 100 career games without batting?

37. Before Reggie Jackson passed him, who was the career strikeout king?

38. Name one of the two players who played in the majors in five different decades.

39. Name one of the two players who hit for the cycle three times.

40. Who played the most consecutive years for the same team?

41. Who had the most RBIs in a single game?

42. Name the last .400 hitter in the National League.

43. Who holds the record for most hits in a season?

44. Who hit the most career grand slams?

45. Whose career home-run record was erased by Babe Ruth in 1921?

46. Who holds the record for the highest batting average in a season in the twentieth century?

47. Who struck out the most times in a season?

48. Name the only teammates with simultaneous 50-homer seasons.

49. What were the original positions of Hank Aaron, Carl Yastrzemski, and Tim Raines?

50. Name the only player to get exactly 3,000 hits.

51. Who hit the most pinch homers in a season?

52. Name the last NL Triple Crown winner.

53. Who was the only player to hit 50 homers for two different teams?

54. Who holds the major-league record for RBIs in a season?

55. Name the only brothers to hit consecutive home runs.

56. Who was the one-armed outfielder who played during World War II?

57. Name the only brothers to win batting titles.

58. Who was the only AL player to have two three-homer games in a season?

59. Who was the oldest player to appear in a major-league game?

60. Name two players who hit five home runs in one day.

One of the few beacons in the fog for the early Padres was slugging first baseman Nate Colbert.

61. Who hit in 72 of 73 games?

62. Who holds the major-league record for stolen bases in a season?

63. Who homered in his first two major-league at-bats?

64. Who pinch hit for both Roger Maris and Ted Williams?

65. Name the only player to lead both leagues in stolen bases.

66. Name two players who homered in eight straight games.

67. What two men led the league in homers and steals in one season?

68. Name at least three players who had three-homer games in both leagues.

69. Who got three hits in an inning?

70. Who got 3,000 hits without a 200-hit season?

71. What batting champion had the lowest average?

72. What AL batting king had only one .300 season?

73. Why was Charlie Maxwell known as a Sunday hitter?

74. How many grand slams did Roger Maris hit in 1961?

75. Who had the longest rookie batting streak?

76. Who hit the most rookie home runs?

77. What family had the most brothers in the majors?

78. Who had the highest career batting average of all time?

79. Who had the best career ratio of home runs per at-bats?

80. How many players have hit 500 homers?

81. Name two of the five players who have appeared in 3,000 games.

82. Of the 16 players with 3,000 hits, three are not in Cooperstown. Name them.

83. He is the only player to hit 100 homers for three different teams.

84. Who had the most homers in a season without 100 runs batted in?

85. He was the only man to homer for teams in all four divisions in one year.

86. Name the only man with at least four 30-homer seasons in both leagues.

87. Whose bout with mental illness was featured in the film *Fear Strikes Out*?

88. Name the only brothers to finish first and second in a batting race.

89. Who hit the most career pinch homers?

90. What former Dodger first baseman became TV's "Rifleman"?

91. Name the only man to hit two grand slams in a game off one pitcher.

92. Who holds the major-league record for stealing without getting caught?

93. Who hit the most grand slams in a season?

94. Name the only pair of teammates to hit 30 homers and steal 30 bases in the same season.

95. They share the record for home runs by an NL rookie.

96. This active player is the career leader in getting hit by a pitch.

97. Who holds the AL record for strikeouts by a hitter in a season?

98. What major-league catcher was an American spy during World War II?

99. Who received the most intentional walks in a season?

100. Who was the first American League pitcher to appear in the starting lineup as a designated hitter?

101. Name the only man to hit three home runs in an Opening Day game.

102. Who knocked in both American League runs in the 1988 All-Star Game?

103. Name the active player who had two straight 100-RBI seasons after replacing a seven-time batting king.

104. Who was baseball's toughest strikeout?

105. Who was the only man to play in baseball's first game and also in the modern era?

106. How did baseball cost Jim Thorpe his Olympic medals?

107. Who was the first man to hit pinch homers in both games of a doubleheader?

108. Name the 1972 AL batting king who failed to hit a home run that year.

109. Who was the first player to earn $2 million a year?

110. According to Ted Williams, why is hitting the toughest job in sports?

• ANSWERS •

1. Everett Scott, who played in 1,307 consecutive games as a shortstop for the Red Sox and Yankees, held the record for consecutive games until passed by Gehrig, the Yankees' Iron Horse. Gehrig went on to play in 2,130 straight games.

2. Hank Aaron and Eddie Mathews of the Braves combined for a record 863 home runs as teammates, 1954–66.

3. Hank Aaron and brother Tommie combined for a record 768 home runs, 755 by Henry and 13 by his brother.

The Aaron brothers, Hank (left) and Tommie, were teammates on the Milwaukee Braves for several seasons.

4. On July 3, 1966, pitcher Tony Cloninger of the Atlanta Braves became the only National Leaguer to hit two grand slams in a game. Cloninger, who also had an RBI single, led the Braves to a 17–3 victory at Candlestick Park.

5. Bob Horner, Dave Winfield, and Pete Incaviglia are active major leaguers who bypassed the minors in going from college to the pros.

6. Ralph Kiner of the Pirates led or tied for NL home-run leadership from 1946 through 1952.

7. Because Mickey Mantle was batting behind him, Maris failed to receive a single intentional walk during his record 61-homer season.

8. Harmon Killebrew came up to the majors as a second baseman, returned to the minors, and eventually returned at third base. He played 11 games at second base, 792 at third, 470 in left field, and 969 at first base.

9. Ed Delahanty of the Phillies and Bob Horner of the Atlanta Braves both hit four homers in games their teams lost.

10. Joe Adcock of the Milwaukee Braves hit four homers and a double at Brooklyn's Ebbets Field on July 31, 1954.

11. Manny Mota produced a record 150 career pinch hits.

Manny Mota was an expert at producing in pressure situations.

12. Red Schoendienst missed virtually all of the 1959 season, while Rico Carty was idled with TB in 1968.

13. Ty Cobb (three times) and Tim Raines. Cobb's statistics in one of those years, 1911, included a .420 batting average, 83 stolen bases, 144 runs batted in, 147 runs scored, and 248 hits, including 24 triples.

14. Mike Schmidt of the Phillies, on July 17, 1976, and Bob Horner, then of the Braves, on July 6, 1986.

15. Jose Canseco of the Oakland Athletics did it in 1988.

16. Pete Rose was a rookie second baseman with the Reds in 1963.

17. The 1973 Atlanta Braves.

18. Dave Johnson (43), Darrell Evans (41), and Hank Aaron (40) are the only trio of teammates to enjoy simultaneous 40-homer seasons.

19. Steve Garvey (33), Reggie Smith (32), and Dusty Baker and Ron Cey (30 each) gave the Dodgers the only quartet of 30-homer teammates in major-league history.

20. Felipe, Matty, and Jesus Alou hit consecutive groundouts, accounting for all three outs in a 1–2–3 inning for the Giants during a 1963 game against the Mets at Shea Stadium.

21. Among current big leaguers whose dads played in the majors are Barry Bonds, son of Bobby; Buddy Bell, son of Gus; Bob Boone, son of Ray; Joel Skinner, son of Bob; Stan Javier, son of Julian; Vance Law, son of Vern; Danny Tartabull, son of Jose; Ozzie Virgil, son of Ozzie; Steve Trout, son of Dizzy; Terry Kennedy, son of Bob;

Dick Schofield, son of Dick; and Kurt Stillwell, son of Ron.

22. On June 8, 1961, Eddie Mathews, Hank Aaron, Joe Adcock, and Frank Thomas of the Braves hit consecutive homers against the Reds in the seventh inning. Cincinnati eventually won the game, 10–8.

23. When the Cleveland Indians duplicated the four-consecutive-homer feat on July 31,1963, they did it with the 8–9–1–2 hitters: Woodie Held, pitcher Pedro Ramos, Tito Francona, and Larry Brown. The Minnesota Twins also produced four straight homers, on May 2, 1964. The batters were Tony Oliva, Bob Allison, Jimmie Hall, and Harmon Killebrew. They connected against the Kansas City Athletics in the 11th inning.

24. Bert Campaneris did it for the Kansas Athletics in 1965 and Cesar Tovar for the Minnesota Twins in 1968. Tovar, who started the game as the pitcher, struck out Reggie Jackson during his one-inning stint.

25. Rennie Stennett of the Pirates went 7 for 7 against the Cubs on September 16, 1975. The Pirates won, 22–0. Cesar Gutierrez of the Tigers also went 7 for 7 during the modern era, although it was in a 12-inning game, on June 21, 1970. In the last century, Wilbert Robinson of the Baltimore Orioles went 7 for 7 in a regulation game on June 10, 1892.

26. George Foster of the Reds hit 52 in 1977.

27. Larry Doby, one of 14 blacks signed by Bill Veeck's Cleveland Indians in the early years of integrated baseball, became the American League's first black player late in the 1947 season.

28.   Bobby Bonds was in the 30/30 Club a record six times, twice in the NL and four times in the AL.

Bobby Bonds displayed a rare combination of speed and power for several teams, starting with the San Francisco Giants.

29.   Darrell Evans hit 41 home runs for the 1973 Braves and 40 for the 1985 Tigers.

30.   Cy Williams of the Phillies was 40 when he hit 30 homers, tying Hack Wilson for NL leadership, in 1927. Both were overlooked when AL leader Babe Ruth hit 60 that year.

31.   Ray Chapman of the Indians was struck by a pitch thrown by Carl Mays of the Yankees during a game in 1920. He died of head injuries a day later.

32.   Mike Schmidt of the Phillies hit 48 in 1980. Eddie Mathews, the previous record holder, hit 47 in 1953.

33.   Hack Wilson of the Cubs hit an NL record 56 homers in 1930.

34.   Hank Aaron, 755, Babe Ruth, 714, Willie Mays, 660.

35.   Ron Blomberg of the Yankees on April 6, 1973. He went 1 for 3 in a game his team lost to the Red Sox, 15–5.

36. Herb Washington got into 105 games, spread over two seasons, without coming to bat for the Oakland Athletics. A Michigan State track star, Washington was used strictly as a pinch runner in 92 games for the World Champion A's of 1974. He stole 31 bases in 48 attempts and scored 33 runs. He also appeared in three games of the World Series against the Los Angeles Dodgers. Maverick owner Charles O. Finley was the man who came up with the idea of signing the running specialist.

37. Willie Stargell was the career strikeout king before Reggie Jackson.

Longtime Pittsburgh star Willie Stargell was not known only for hitting home runs.

38. Nick Altrock (1898–1933) and Minnie Minoso (1949–80).

39. Bob Meusel of the Yankees in 1921–22–28 and Babe Herman of the Dodgers in 1931 (twice) and for the Cubs in 1933.

40. Carl Yastrzemski played 23 consecutive seasons with the Red Sox. Brooks Robinson spent 23 straight years with the Orioles. Cap Anson, who played 22 straight years with the Cubs, holds the NL record.

41. On September 16, 1924, Jim Bottomley of the Cardinals went 6 for 6 against Brooklyn with two home runs, a double, and 12 runs batted in.

42. Bill Terry of the New York Giants hit .401 in 1930.

43. George Sisler of the St. Louis Browns had 257 hits in 1920.

44. Lou Gehrig hit 23 career grand slams, all for the Yankees.

45. Roger Connor had been the lifetime home-run king with 138 until Ruth surpassed that career total in 1921 (Gavvy Cravath had been the modern-era leader with 119). Connor had three homers in an 1888 game, a 6 for 6 game in 1895, and 12 .300 seasons.

46. Rogers Hornsby ranks first in the modern era with a .424 mark in 1924. Hugh Duffy holds the all-time record with a .438 average in 1894.

47. Bobby Bonds whiffed a record 189 times for the 1970 Giants.

48. Yankee teammates Roger Maris (61) and Mickey Mantle (54) in 1961.

Roger Maris (left) and Mickey Mantle provided a devastating one-two punch for the Yankees of the early 1960s.

49. Second base.

50. Roberto Clemente, a 13-time .300 hitter, reached the 3,000-hit plateau at the end of the 1972 season but lost his life in a plane crash on New Year's Eve of that year. He had been ferrying relief supplies to earthquake victims in Nicaragua.

51. Johnny Frederick of the 1932 Brooklyn Dodgers hit six.

52. Joe Medwick of the Cardinals hit .374 with 31 homers and 154 RBI in 1937.

53. Jimmie Foxx hit 58 for the 1932 Athletics and 50 for the 1938 Red Sox.

54. Hack Wilson of the 1930 Cubs had a major-league record 190 RBI.

55. On September 15, 1938, brothers Lloyd and Paul Waner hit consecutive home runs for Pittsburgh against Cliff Melton of the New York Giants in the fifth inning. Lloyd, who hit only 27 in his 18-year career, never hit another. His total for 1938 was five.

56. Pete Gray hit .218 in 77 games for the St. Louis Browns in 1945, when wartime manpower shortages were acute throughout baseball.

57. Dixie Walker's .357 average led the NL in 1944, while Harry Walker led the league with a .363 mark three years later. Dixie did it for Brooklyn, while Harry split his season between the Phillies and Cardinals.

58. Ted Williams of the Red Sox did it in 1957. NL players who have enjoyed two three-homer games in a season include Willie Stargell, Johnny Mize, Ralph Kiner, and Willie Mays.

59. Satchel Paige was 59 when he pitched three innings for the Kansas City Athletics against the

Red Sox in 1965. He yielded only one hit, a double by Carl Yastrzemski.

60. Stan Musial of the Cardinals homered five times in a doubleheader against the New York Giants in 1954. Nate Colbert of the Padres duplicated the feat in a 1972 twinbill against the Atlanta Braves. Colbert had a record 13 RBI for the day.

61. Joe DiMaggio of the Yankees hit in 72 of 73 games in 1941. After his record hitting streak was stopped at 56 games, DiMaggio immediately launched a 16-game streak.

62. Rickey Henderson, then with the Oakland Athletics, stole 130 bases in 1982 to eclipse Lou Brock's 1974 record of 118 steals in a season.

63. Bob Nieman of the St. Louis Browns homered in his first two major-league at-bats, on September 14, 1951.

64. Carroll Hardy, a lifetime .225 hitter, was a rookie when he pinch hit for Roger Maris while with Cleveland in 1958. He delivered a three-run homer. Called upon to bat for Williams while with the Red Sox on September 20, 1960, Hardy lined into a double play. Williams had yielded his turn at-bat after fouling a ball off his ankle.

65. Ron LeFlore led both leagues in stolen bases. He swiped 68 for Detroit to lead the AL in 1978, and then 97 for the 1980 Montreal Expos.

66. Dale Long did it for Pittsburgh in 1956 and Don Mattingly for the Yankees in 1987.

67. The only men to lead their league in both home runs and stolen bases were Ty Cobb of the 1909 Tigers (nine homers, 76 steals) and Chuck Klein of the 1932 Phillies (38 homers, tying Mel Ott of the New York Giants, and 20 steals).

68. Johnny Mize was the only man to hit three consecutive homers in a game in both leagues. He did it for the 1938 and 1940 Cardinals, 1947 New York Giants, and 1950 Yankees. He also had nonconsecutive three-homer games for the Cardinals in 1938 and 1940. Others with three-homer games in both leagues are Claudell Washington, Larry Parrish, Dave Kingman, and Babe Ruth.

69. Gene Stephens of the Red Sox got three hits in an inning against Detroit on June 18, 1953. He singled twice and doubled once in a 17-run Boston outburst.

70. Carl Yastrzemski.

71. Carl Yastrzemski hit .301 for the 1968 Red Sox.

72. Norm Cash of the Tigers hit .361 in the diluted-pitching expansion year of 1961 but had no other .300 seasons.

73. Maxwell hit 40 of his 148 career homers on Sunday. In 1959 his Sunday production was 12 of 31. He hit four in a 1959 Sunday doubleheader against the Yankees and three in a 1962 doubleheader, also against the Yankees. He played most of his career for Detroit, but also was employed by the Red Sox, Orioles, and White Sox.

74. None.

75. Benito Santiago of the Padres hit in a rookie record 34 straight games near the end of the 1987 season.

76. Mark McGwire of the Oakland Athletics hit 49 home runs in 1987. No previous rookie had hit more than 38.

77. The Delahantys had five brothers in the majors, though never more than three at one time.

78. Ty Cobb's .367 average tops the career list.

79. Babe Ruth hit a home run every 11.76 at-bats.

80. Fourteen, including the still-active Mike Schmidt.

81. Players who have appeared in at least 3,000 games are Pete Rose, Hank Aaron, Stan Musial, Ty Cobb, and Carl Yastrzemski.

82. Carl Yastrzemski, Rod Carew, and Pete Rose have 3,000 hits but are not yet in the Hall of Fame.

83. Reggie Jackson topped 100 homers for the A's, Angels, and Yankees.

84. Harmon Killebrew had 45 homers but only 96 RBI for the 1963 Twins.

85. Dave Kingman homered for the Mets, Padres, Angels, and Yankees in 1977.

86. Frank Robinson.

87. Jimmy Piersall.

88. Matty Alou of the Pirates hit .342 and Felipe Alou of the Braves hit .327 to finish one-two in the 1966 NL batting derby.

89. Cliff Johnson hit 20 pinch-hit homers in his career.

90. Chuck Connors.

91. On July 27, 1946, Rudy York of the Red Sox hit a pair of grand-slam home runs off Tex Shirley of the St. Louis Browns.

92. Davey Lopes of the Dodgers swiped 38 straight bases in 1975.

93. Don Mattingly of the Yankees hit six in 1987.

94. Howard Johnson and Darryl Strawberry of the Mets became the first teammates to join the 30/30 Club, in 1987.

95. Frank Robinson of the 1956 Reds and Wally Berger of the 1930 Braves share the record for home runs by a National League rookie. Each hit 38.

Don Baylor, who played for several clubs, has a reputation for crowding the plate.

96. Don Baylor.

97. Rob Deer of the Brewers struck out 186 times in 1987.

Brewers outfielder Rob Deer made the record books in 1987.

98. Moe Berg, who spent 15 years in the majors, was a Princeton graduate who could speak 16

different languages. Sent to Japan with the Babe Ruth All-Stars in 1934, Berg took secret pictures that were used by General Jimmie Doolittle when he bombed Tokyo in 1942. Later, Berg joined the O.S.S. and was sent behind Nazi lines to learn about German atomic bomb experiments. His exploits were documented in several books.

99. Willie McCovey of the Giants was intentionally walked 45 times in 1969.

100. Rick Rhoden of the New York Yankees was used as a starting DH by Billy Martin early in the 1988 season.

101. George Bell of the Toronto Blue Jays did it in 1988.

102. Terry Steinbach, catcher for the Oakland Athletics, had a home run and sacrifice fly as his team won, 2–1, at Cincinnati's Riverfront Stadium.

103. Wally Joyner, who replaced Rod Carew as first baseman of the Angels in 1986.

104. Joe Sewell, a left-handed hitting shortstop who hit .312 in a career that stretched from 1920 to 1933, holds several records that reflect his excellent bat control. They include most consecutive games without striking out (115 in 1929), fewest strikeouts in a season (4 in both 1925 and 1929), and fewest strikeouts in a career (114 in 1,903 games over 14 seasons). Sewell, a member of the Hall of Fame, spent most of his playing time with the Cleveland Indians.

105. Catcher Jim (Orator) O'Rourke played for Boston against Philadelphia on April 22, 1876, when National League play began, and was a 52-year-old minor-league manager in 1904

when he got another chance to play in the majors. John McGraw, manager of the New York Giants, agreed to O'Rourke's request that he be allowed to play in the majors one last time. On September 22, O'Rourke played in the opener of a doubleheader against Cincinnati and got a hit, helping the Giants clinch the NL pennant with a 7–5 victory.

106.   Jim Thorpe, who played for three major-league teams in a brief big-league career, won two Gold Medals at the 1912 Olympics but lost them six months later when the U.S. Amateur Athletic Committee ruled he was not an amateur. The committee learned that Thorpe had accepted two dollars a day to play baseball in a North Carolina summer league before the Olympics. Thorpe claimed he was a simple Indian schoolboy who did not know the rules. Thorpe's medals were restored posthumously in 1982 after the International Olympic Committee accepted official requests for restoration by the Amateur Athletic Union and the U.S. Olympic Committee.

107.   Joe Cronin of the Red Sox hit two pinch homers on June 17, 1943.

108.   Rod Carew.

109.   According to baseball's Player Relations Committee, George Foster was the first to reach that plateau.

110.   "It is very difficult," said Williams, "to swing a round bat at a round ball and hit it square."

• 2 •
PITCHERS

Baseball insiders suggest pitching is 75 to 90 percent of the game. Light-hitting teams with good pitching, backed by good defense and often good speed, have won pennants, while heavy-hitting teams with weak pitching haven't.

In 1930, for example, the Philadelphia Phillies had a team batting average of .315, with eight regulars over .300. Yet the club lost 102 games and finished last because its pitchers allowed opponents to score a record average of 6.71 earned runs a game.

As the late Walter Alston, long-time manager of the Dodgers, explained: "When you get consistently good pitching, you keep the score low and have a chance in every game. You can try to use all the ways there are to score a run and benefit from any error or lucky break. You're never out of the game.

"If, on the other hand, your pitching gives up lots of runs, there will be times when you're out of business early, where the only way to get back is with a lot of slugging of your own. So it's pretty hard to be lucky when your pitching is bad."

Good control and variety of pitches are hallmarks of baseball's best pitchers. When Cy Young, the career leader in victories, pitched for the 1904 Red Sox, he walked just 28 batters in 380 innings. Nearly 30 years later, Carl Hubbell of the New York Giants showed impeccable control during an 18-inning 1–0 victory over the Cardinals: he didn't walk a batter.

The postwar development of relief pitching changed the way managers handle their pitching staffs but only increased the importance of the man on the mound.

• SCORING •

Scoring this one should be simple. Use the following Passaic High School rules:

90–100   Grade A. You've mastered the split-fingered fastball.

80–89   Grade B. You throw a mean curveball.

70–79   Grade C. Work on your control.

60–69   Grade D. Never walk the leadoff hitter.

Under 60   Grade F. Mop-up man at best.

• QUESTIONS •

1. Name the youngest pitcher to hurl a no-hitter.

2. Who was the last pitcher to throw the spitball legally?

3. What pitcher had the highest batting average in a season?

4. Who pitched the only Opening Day no-hitter?

5. Who pitched the most no-hitters?

6. What brother tandem has the most career victories?

7. Who won more games than any other left-hander?

8. Who pitched a record 59 consecutive scoreless innings?

9. Who homered twice while pitching a no-hitter?

10. Name at least two pitchers who won 100 games in both leagues.

11. Name at least two pitchers who pitched no-hitters in both leagues.

12. Who pitched 12 perfect innings only to lose in the 13th?

13. What star pitcher attacked John Roseboro with a bat?

14. Whose one-hitter was caught by Dale Murphy?

15. Whom did Ronald Reagan portray in *A Winning Team*?

16. Name the first winner of the Cy Young Award.

17. Name the last 30-game winner before Denny McLain went 31–6 in 1968.

18. Who lost the most games lifetime?

19. Who lost the most games in a season?

20. Who holds the record for relief losses in a season?

21. Who won the most games in a season?

22. Name the two pitchers who topped 400 career wins.

23. What strikeout artist was struck in the eye by Gil McDougald's liner?

24. Whose 9-0 record after his August arrival by trade helped his team top the AL East in 1987?

25. Who pitched a major-league record 12 one-hitters?

26. What pitcher was the youngest player in major-league history?

27. What pitcher homered three times in a game?

28. Who pitched three complete-game double-headers?

29. What team handed Pittsburgh reliever Elroy Face his only defeat after 17 straight wins in 1959?

30. Their refusal to sign reserve-clause contracts sparked the free-agent revolution of 1976. Name these two pitchers.

31. Who holds the major-league record for most games pitched?

32. Name the only NL pitcher to work at least 100 games in a season.

33. Name Steve Carlton's last major league team.

34. Name three pitchers who have had 45-save seasons.

35. Who threw the eephus pitch?

36. Name the only pitcher to throw consecutive no-hitters.

37. What was unusual about the 5–19 record Virgil Trucks posted for the 1952 Tigers?

38. Who pitched the last no-hitter against the Yankees?

39. What pitcher struck out 19 hitters in a losing effort?

40. What pitcher holds the major-league record for strikeouts in a game?

41. What is the major-league record for strikeouts in a nine-inning game?

42. Who pitched a perfect game that was not a complete game?

43. Who pitched a complete game without getting a decision?

44. Name the only man to lose a nine-inning no-hitter.

45. What pair of brothers pitched no-hitters?

46. Name the only brothers to pitch a combined shutout.

47. What two pitchers worked the 1965 game in which the teams combined for one hit?

48. Who holds the single-season strikeout record?

49. Who pitched to Babe Ruth and Mickey Mantle?

50. What three Mikes beat Ron Guidry in the 1978 season?

51. Who yielded Joe Niekro's only career homer?

52. Name the only player to catch no-hitters by Nolan Ryan and Sandy Koufax.

53. Who threw a no-hitter in his first start?

54. Who yielded Hank Aaron's last home run?

55. Who yielded the most home runs in a season?

56. Who was the oldest pitcher to win a game?

57. Name the two pitchers who have 4,000 strike-outs.

58. Who started the most openers?

59. Who started the most consecutive openers?

60. Name the only pitcher to yield four straight homers in an inning.

61. What pitcher won the most games without pitching a no-hitter?

62. What one-armed pitcher hurled a no-hitter?

63. Who struck out the most hitters during a no-hitter?

64. Name the only pitcher whose no-hitter clinched a pennant.

65. Who was the oldest pitcher to throw a no-hit game?

66. Who was the last pitcher to throw a perfect game?

67. Who was the last pitcher to win and lose 20 games in one season?

68. Who yielded Babe Ruth's 60th homer in 1927?

69. Name the only pitcher to win ERA titles in three different decades.

70. Who yielded the hit that enabled Pete Rose to top Ty Cobb as the career base-hit leader?

71. Name the only pitcher to beat the Braves in three different cities.

72. Who was the last pitcher to lose 200 without winning that many?

73. Who holds the record for strikeouts by a rookie pitcher?

74. Who holds the record for saves by a rookie reliever?

75. What rookie won the most games?

76. What is the record for consecutive games pitched?

77. What two pitchers threw gopher balls to Hank Aaron in both leagues?

78. Who pitched a no-hitter for the Mets?

79. Who holds the record for home runs by a pitcher in a season?

80. What pitcher hit the most career home runs?

81. Name the youngest 20-game winner.

82. What rookie pitched the most shutouts?

83. Who saved the most games lifetime?

84. Name the last AL pitcher to hit a regular-season home run.

85. Did two pitchers ever no-hit each other for nine innings?

86. Why was 1968 called "The Year of the Pitcher"?

87. Name the Tiger rookie who outpitched Bob Feller to win the 1940 flag for Detroit by one game over Cleveland.

88. What bespectacled Yankee reliever intimidated opponents with a blazing fastball, a penchant for wildness, and poor eyesight?

89. Who pitched a perfect game on Father's Day?

90. Only two pitchers have hurled four or more no-hitters. Name them.

91. This pitcher won four Cy Young Awards but never pitched a no-hitter.

92. What AL pitcher homered two years after the institution of the designated-hitter rule?

93. Why were left-handed pitchers scarce when baseball began?

94. Why was Ted Lyons known as a Sunday pitcher?

95. Who started Opening Day games for both Washington teams?

96. Who pitched for the Seattle Pilots and Seattle Mariners?

97. After these two pitchers, Boston Brave fans prayed for rain.

98. This reliever for the pennant-winning 1961 Reds became a respected baseball author after he left the game.

99. Name two Yale alumni who have pitched for the Mets.

100. Name the two Milwaukee pitchers who no-hit the Phillies in 1960.

• ANSWERS •

1. Nick Maddox was 20 when he pitched a 1907 no-hitter for Pittsburgh. He was a few months younger than Bob Feller was when the Cleveland great recorded the first of his three no-hitters.

2. Burleigh Grimes was one of 17 pitchers allowed to continue throwing the spitball after it was banned in 1920. Grimes retired in 1934.

3. Walter Johnson hit .404 for the 1925 Senators.

4. Bob Feller defeated the Chicago White Sox,

1-0, on April 16, 1940. It was the only complete-game no-hitter ever pitched on Opening Day.

5. Nolan Ryan has pitched five no-hitters.

6. Phil Niekro, who retired after the 1987 season, and brother Joe surpassed Jim and Gaylord Perry for victories by brothers. The Niekros had 538 wins between them as the 1988 season began.

7. Warren Spahn's 363 wins, mostly for the Boston and Milwaukee Braves, are the most by a left-hander.

8. Orel Hershiser of the Los Angeles Dodgers broke Don Drysdale's record (set in 1968) of 58-2/3 scoreless innings on the last day of the 1988 season.

9. Rick Wise of the Phillies homered twice during his June 23, 1971, no-hit win over Cincinnati. The score was 4-0.

10. Pitchers with at least 100 wins in both leagues include Cy Young, Jim Bunning, Nolan Ryan, Ferguson Jenkins, and Gaylord Perry.

Ferguson Jenkins was a star pitcher in both leagues.

11. Nolan Ryan, Jim Bunning, and Cy Young authored no-hitters in both leagues.

12.   Harvey Haddix hurled 12 perfect innings for Pittsburgh against the Milwaukee Braves on May 26, 1959, then lost a 1-0 decision in the 13th. The only hit, initially thought to be a home run by Joe Adcock, was declared a double when Adcock accidentally passed teammate Hank Aaron on the base paths.

13.   Juan Marichal of the Giants attacked John Roseboro of the Dodgers with a bat while at the plate during a 1965 game. Dodger pitcher Sandy Koufax attempted to play peacemaker in the fight, precipitated when Marichal thought Roseboro was throwing too close to his head when returning the ball to Koufax.

14.   Phil Niekro pitched a one-hitter caught by Murphy when the future two-time MVP first came up to the Braves. Murphy, once re-garded as "the next Johnny Bench," became a star outfielder later.

15.   Grover Cleveland Alexander.

16.   Don Newcombe of the Brooklyn Dodgers in 1956. At the time, the award was given to only one major-league pitcher each year.

Don Newcombe of the Brooklyn Dodgers was a good hitter as well as a good pitcher.

17. Dizzy Dean, 30–4 for the 1934 Cardinals.

18. Cy Young lost a major-league record 313 games.

19. Vic Willis, a 29-game loser for the 1905 Boston Braves, has been the biggest one-season loser. He won 11 games that year, during which he suffered from nonsupport; his ERA was a respectable 3.21.

20. Gene Garber went 6–16 for the Atlanta Braves in 1979.

21. Jack Chesbro of the New York Highlanders won 41 and lost 12 in 1904.

22. Cy Young (511) and Walter Johnson (416).

23. Herb Score of the Indians was injured when McDougald, the second batter up for the Yankees in the first inning of the May 7, 1957, game, hit him with a line drive. Score, a 20-game winner the year before, suffered a broken bone and eye damage and was never again the same pitcher. He retired in 1962 at age 29.

24. Doyle Alexander was traded to the Detroit Tigers by the Atlanta Braves. The trade helped the Tigers to beat another of Alexander's former teams, the Toronto Blue Jays, to the division title.

25. Bob Feller.

Bob Feller's fastball frustrated rival hitters so frequently that he threw three no-hitters and a record 12 one-hitters.

26. Joe Nuxhall, Reds, was 15 when he made his debut on June 10, 1944. He pitched two-thirds of an inning in an 18-0 loss to St. Louis.

27. Jim Tobin, Boston Braves, beat the Cubs, 6–5, when he homered three times on May 13, 1942. He had six home runs that year and 17 in his career, which spanned 796 at-bats.

28. Joe (Iron Man) McGinnity, New York Giants, in 1903.

29. The Los Angeles Dodgers were the only team to beat Face in 1959. He finished the season at 18–1.

30. Andy Messersmith and Dave McNally.

Two members of the pitching fraternity who shared a common destiny were Andy Messersmith (reading) and Dave McNally.

31. Reliever Hoyt Wilhelm pitched in 1,070 games.

32. Mike Marshall made a record 106 appearances for the 1974 Los Angeles Dodgers. Marshall also holds the AL record for games pitched in a season, 90 with the 1979 Minnesota Twins.

33. The 1988 Minnesota Twins.

34.   Dave Righetti (46) and Bruce Sutter and Dan Quisenberry (45 each).

35.   Rip Sewell of the Pirates developed the high, arcing pitch after a friend accidentally fired buckshot into his foot on the last day of the 1941 hunting season. Favoring the foot, Sewell adopted the delivery that produced the pitch, dubbed the eephus by outfielder Maurice Van Robays. Ted Williams hit a celebrated three-run homer on an eephus during the 1946 All-Star Game.

36.   Johnny Vander Meer of the Reds no-hit the Boston Braves and Brooklyn Dodgers on June 11 and 15, 1938. The second no-hitter was also the first night game at Ebbets Field.

37.   Two of his victories were no-hitters.

38.   Hoyt Wilhelm of the Orioles, in a rare start, on September 20, 1958.

39.   Steve Carlton of the Cardinals, on September 15, 1969, against the Mets. Ron Swoboda's pair of two-run homers gave New York a 4–3 victory.

40.   Tom Cheney of the Senators fanned 21 batters in a 16-inning game against the Red Sox on September 12, 1962.

41.   Roger Clemens of the Red Sox fanned 20 Mariners on April 29, 1986.

42.   Ernie Shore of the Red Sox relieved Babe Ruth in the first inning on June 17, 1917, after Ruth had been ejected for arguing a "ball four" call on the leadoff man. The runner was erased trying to steal, and Shore proceeded to retire the next 26 men in order. He got credit for a perfect game because he recorded 27 outs without a hit, walk, or error, but it was not a complete game.

43. Warren Spahn, as a 1942 rookie with the Boston Braves, was pitching the nightcap of a Polo Grounds doubleheader on September 26 when hundreds of fans spilled onto the field. Although trailing 5–2 in the eighth inning, Spahn escaped a certain loss when umpire Ziggy Sears forfeited the game to the Braves. Forfeits are recorded as 9–0 victories without winning or losing pitchers. Other batting and pitching records count, however. Spahn got credit for a complete game but finished the year with a 0–0 record in four appearances.

44. Ken Johnson of the Houston Colt .45s lost a 1–0 decision to the Reds on April 23, 1964, on his own ninth-inning error. In the final frame, Pete Rose bunted, reached second on Johnson's throwing error, moved to third on a grounder, and scored on an error by Nelson Fox.

45. Ken Forsch of the Astros and Bob Forsch of the Cardinals both pitched no-hitters. Bob no-hit the Phils on April 16, 1978, and Ken throttled the Braves on April 7, 1979.

46. Rick and Paul Reuschel of the Cubs combined to blank the Dodgers on August 21, 1975. Rick went the first 6-1/3 innings.

47. Sandy Koufax of the Dodgers pitched a perfect game to beat the Cubs, 1–0, but Chicago's Bobby Hendley yielded only a Lou Johnson single. The Dodgers scored when Johnson walked, was bunted to second, stole third, and scored on a high throw by catcher Chris Krug.

48. Nolan Ryan fanned 383 hitters, one more than Sandy Koufax, for the single-season record. Ryan accomplished the feat with the Angels in 1973.

49. Al Benton was with the Philadelphia Athletics when he faced Ruth in 1934 and with the Red Sox when he faced Mantle in 1952.

50. Mike Caldwell of the Brewers; Mike Flanagan of the Orioles; Mike Willis of the Blue Jays.

51. Brother Phil, the victim, lost a 4–3 game when Joe homered for Houston in the seventh inning on May 29, 1976.

52. Jeff Torborg.

53. Bobo Holloman of the Browns blanked the Philadelphia Athletics, 6–0, in his starting debut on May 6, 1953. He had made four previous relief outings. Flushed with success, Holloman never pitched another complete game. He was sent to the minors with a 3–7 record on July 23 and never returned.

54. Dick Drago, pitching for the Angels, on July 20, 1976.

55. Bert Blyleven of the Twins gave up 50 in 1986.

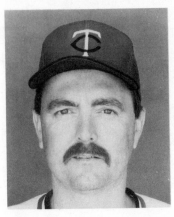

Minnesota's Bert Blyleven is one of the game's best pitchers because of his curveball.

56. Phil Niekro of the Indians was 48 when he won a game on July 20, 1987.

57. Nolan Ryan and Steve Carlton.

Knuckleball specialist Phil Niekro showed the Indians that life begins after 40.

58. Tom Seaver pitched 16 openers, 11 for the Mets, 3 for the Reds, and 2 for the White Sox.

59. Robin Roberts pitched 12 straight for the Phils, 1950–61.

60. Paul Foytack of the Angels retired the first two batters in the sixth inning of the July 31, 1963, game, before Cleveland's 8-9-1-2 hitters homered consecutively. They were, in order: Woodie Held, pitcher Pedro Ramos, Tito Francona, and Larry Brown.

61. Grover Cleveland Alexander, 373.

62. Hugh Daily of the Cleveland NL team beat Philadelphia, 1–0, on September 13, 1883.

63. Nolan Ryan of the Angels whiffed 17 Tigers during his July 15, 1973, no-hitter, winning 6–0.

64. Mike Scott of the Astros fanned 13 while beating the Giants 2–0 in a pennant-clinching no-hitter on September 25, 1986.

65. Cy Young was 41 years and three months old when he beat the New York Highlanders 8–0 for the Red Sox on June 30, 1908. Warren Spahn was the only other 40-year-old to pitch a no-hitter, in 1961.

66. Mike Witt of the Angels threw a perfect game at the Texas Rangers on September 30, 1984, the last day of the season.

67. Phil Niekro of the Braves went 21–20 in 1979 to lead the NL in both departments.

68. Tom Zachary of the Senators.

69. Warren Spahn led in ERA in 1947 (2.33), 1953 (2.10), and 1961 (3.01).

70. Eric Show of the Padres, on September 11, 1985. Rose got his 4,192nd career hit in the first inning of the Riverfront Stadium game.

71. Robin Roberts beat the Braves in Boston, Milwaukee, and Atlanta.

72. Bob Friend, whose career record was 197–230.

73. Dwight Gooden of the Mets, 276 in 1984.

Dwight Gooden of the Mets broke into the big leagues with a big season.

74. Todd Worrell of the Cardinals, 36 in 1986.

75. Grover Cleveland Alexander was 28–13 for the 1911 Phillies.

76. Mike Marshall of the Dodgers and Dale Mohorcic of the Rangers both worked in 13 consecu-

tive games for their clubs. Marshall's streak ran from June 18 to July 3, 1974, while Mohorcic's went from August 6 to August 20, 1986.

77. Gaylord Perry and Nolan Ryan.

78. No one has ever pitched a no-hitter for the Mets.

79. Wes Ferrell of the Indians hit nine home runs in 1931.

80. Wes Ferrell, 38.

81. Dwight Gooden of the Mets beat the Padres for his 20th win on August 25, 1985, at age 20 years, nine months, and nine days, a month younger than Bob Feller was when he notched his 20th win in 1939.

82. Fernando Valenzuela of the Dodgers pitched eight shutouts in 1981.

83. Rollie Fingers, 341.

84. Roric Harrison of the Orioles hit the last regular-season homer by an AL pitcher on October 3, 1972.

85. Yes. On May 2,1917, Cincinnati's Fred Toney completed his no-hitter through the 10th inning, when the Reds finally got to Chicago's Jim (Hippo) Vaughn for two hits and an unearned run. Cincinnati won, 1-0.

86. Falling batting averages, a rise in the number of low-scoring games, a total of 335 shut-outs, and spectacular performances by Bob Gibson, Denny McLain, and Don Drysdale made 1968 a pitchers' year. Six AL starters yielded an average of less than two earned runs per game.

87. Floyd Giebell blanked Feller's Indians, 2-0, to help Detroit win the AL pennant by one game over Cleveland. Giebell won just two other games in his career.

88. Ryne Duren.

89. Jim Bunning of the Phillies, against the Mets on June 21, 1964.

90. Nolan Ryan and Sandy Koufax.

91. Steve Carlton.

92. The designated-hitter rule, used only by the American League, allows a player to take the pitcher's batting turn without forcing the pitcher from the game. Because the National League disdains the rule, the commissioner of baseball ruled in 1976 that alternate World Series would include the DH. In 1974, before that ruling, Ken Holtzman of the Oakland Athletics hit a World Series home run against the Los Angeles Dodgers.

93. Late into the nineteenth century, children with a natural inclination to be left-handed were encouraged—often forced physically—to become right-handed instead. Being left-handed was thought to bring bad luck. With a paucity of left-handed youths, baseball was virtually all right-handed during its early days. The first left-handed pitcher, Bobby Mitchell of the Cincinnati Red Stockings, did not reach the National League until 1878, two seasons after the founding of the Senior Circuit.

94. Longtime White Sox starter Ted Lyons got off to a fast start in 1939: with his knuckleball dancing, Lyons started a winning streak after losing his first decision. By chance, most of his starts seemed to fall on Sunday—a combination of scheduling, rainouts, and the coincidence of the team's rotation. Manager Jimmie Dykes, noting the Lyons penchant for Sunday victories, decided to follow the routine regularly. Only

rain on Sunday would change the plan, which gave Lyons more off-days than usual and enabled him to conserve his strength. He went 14-6 (all six losses on the road) with a 2.76 ERA, second in the league, in 1939. He was equally effective during three more years of the Sunday regimen. In his last full year before military service intervened, he went 14-6 with a league-leading 2.10 ERA, completing all 20 of his 1942 starts—a record last achieved by Hall of Famer Walter Johnson, who completed all 29 of his starts in 1918.

95. Camilo Pascual.

96. Diego Segui.

97. Warren Spahn and Johnny Sain.

98. Jim Brosnan wrote the bestselling *The Long Season*.

99. Ken MacKenzie and Ron Darling.

100. Warren Spahn and Lew Burdette.

• 3 •
MANAGERS AND EXECUTIVES

When management, fans, or both are unhappy with the play of a major-league team, the field manager is usually the victim of their wrath. Logically, that makes sense, because it's easier to fire one manager than 24 ballplayers.

Even if a team advances to postseason play, the manager's job is not necessarily safe. The New York Yankees won the 1964 American League pennant but fired manager Yogi Berra anyway; the 1980 Yankees, champions of the AL East, did the same to Dick Howser after a 103-win season.

Casey Stengel got the axe even after winning 10 pennants in 12 years for the Yanks. He was sent packing after Pittsburgh won the 1960 World Series from New York in the last half of the last inning in the last game.

Clubs tend to seek experience in their managers; more than 50 managers since the turn of the century have managed at least three teams each. Jimmie Dykes and Dick Williams managed six different clubs, while Billy Martin has had five different terms as manager of one team: the New York Yankees.

According to Connie Mack, who had 3,776 wins and 4,025 losses during his long managerial career: "Talent comprises 75 percent of managing. Strategy is 12½ percent, and the other 12½ percent is whatever a manager can get out of his team."

Although Mack had the most wins (and the most losses) as a manager, Joe McCarthy had the best winning percentage (.614). McCarthy was also among the select few pilots who produced pennants in both leagues.

Successful managers must establish cordial relations with the media, keep 24 players happy even though nine play at any given time, and argue just enough to placate ownership without angering umpires. It isn't easy.

• SCORING •

Did you manage to get the most out of your baseball acumen in this chapter? Use the following grading guidelines to find out:

45–50	Grade A. You've earned a three-year contract.
40–44	Grade B. Not quite Manager-of-the-Year but close.
35–39	Grade C. You did well with a mediocre ballclub.
30–34	Grade D. On shaky ground.
Under 30	Grade F. Fired by July 4.

• QUESTIONS •

1. Name the only manager to win the World Series in both leagues.

2. Who was the first black manager?

3. Name two other black managers.

4. Name two Cubans who managed in the majors.

5. Who had four terms at the helm of the Pirates?

6. What active NL manager was once general manager of the same team?

7. What active general manager once managed his team?

8. Who managed one team the longest?

9. Who managed the most years without winning a pennant?

10. Name at least three of the five managers who won flags in both leagues.

11. Who devised baseball's signs and signals?

12. Who was the only manager to win pennants with three different teams?

13. Who managed Brooklyn's only World Championship team?

14. Name the first manager of the Mets.

15. What innovative executive pioneered night baseball and plane travel for teams?

16. Who converted Babe Ruth into an outfielder?

17. Who is known as "the father of modern baseball"?

18. Who first developed the farm-system concept?

19. Who devised the Ted Williams shift?

20. Who was the first manager to use a relief pitcher?

21. Name the only man to play, manage, and umpire in the majors.

22. Who was the youngest manager?

23. What playing manager led the league in hitting?

24. Name the first manager to win pennants in both leagues.

25. Name the only postwar Yankee manager who did not manage in Yankee Stadium.

26. Name the only manager of the Seattle Pilots.

27. Who managed the Brooklyn Dodgers in Jackie Robinson's debut?

28. What owner publicly chastised his team for inept play?

29. Name the two managers who had 100-win summers in both leagues.

30. Who was the oldest manager?

31. Why did baseball create the office of commissioner?

32. Who first suggested the designated hitter?

33. Why was Bucky Harris called the "Boy Wonder"?

Longtime manager Bucky Harris spent most of his career managing the Senators.

34. What manager was traded three times?

35. Name two managers who didn't wear uniforms.

36. Why do managers platoon players?

37.   Why do teams use signals?

38.   Who was ejected from a game for sarcastically offering orange juice to the umpires?

39.   Who was responsible for baseball's notorious color line?

40.   Whose televised comments caused baseball to launch a strong push to hire minorities?

41.   What manager twice sent in pinch hitters for pitchers who were pitching no-hitters?

42.   What team operated without a manager?

43.   Why did the Yankees hire Miller Huggins?

Miller Huggins (in uniform) confers with Yankee owner Col. Jacob Ruppert before one of the many World Series games played at the new Yankee Stadium.

44.   Who was "the Mahatma"?

45.   Who was accused of being a push-button manager?

46. What manager was so adept at stealing signs that he told his All-Star squad he'd flash each man the signals used on his own team?

47. Who said, "The Giants is dead. They'll never bother us again"?

48. Who had the most managerial stints with one team?

49. Who managed the Orioles to their 1966 World Series sweep?

50. Who succeeded Dick Williams as manager of the world champion Oakland Athletics?

• ANSWERS •

1. Sparky Anderson won in the AL with the 1984 Tigers and in the NL with the Reds of 1975–76.

Sparky Anderson, who managed the Big Red Machine before shifting to Detroit, has long been regarded as one of baseball's best managers.

2. Frank Robinson, playing manager of the Indians in 1975.

3. Larry Doby, with the 1978 White Sox, and Maury Wills, with the 1980–81 Seattle Mariners.

4. Mike Gonzalez, 1938 Cardinals; Preston Gomez, 1969–70 Padres, 1974 Astros, and 1980 Cubs; and Cookie Rojas, 1988 Angels.

5. Danny Murtaugh.

6. Whitey Herzog, Cardinals.

7. Bobby Cox, Braves.

8. Connie Mack, Philadelphia Athletics, 50 years, 1901–50.

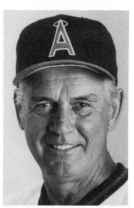

Left: Connie Mack was the manager of the first American League All-Star team in 1933.

Right: Gene Mauch managed the Twins, Expos, and Phillies before spending two terms as manager of the Angels.

9. Gene Mauch, 26 years.

10. Joe McCarthy, Sparky Anderson, Dick Williams, Alvin Dark, and Yogi Berra.

11. When John McGraw and Wee Willie Keeler played together for the National League's Baltimore Orioles during the 1890s, they devised a series of signs that enabled them to surprise opponents with squeeze bunts, hit-and-run plays, and other tactical maneuvers. McGraw later perfected his sign system as the longtime manager of the New York Giants.

12. Bill McKechnie's 25-year managerial career included pennants with the Pirates, Cardinals, and Reds (twice). He retired as an active manager after the 1946 season.

13. Walter Alston in 1955.

14. Casey Stengel.

15. Larry MacPhail brought night baseball to the major leagues with the 1935 Cincinnati Reds. On May 24, 1935, the Reds beat the Phillies, 2–1, in a Crosley Field night game, the first played in the majors. MacPhail, who later instituted night games for the Dodgers and Yankees, also was the first executive to use air travel extensively— with the 1946 Yankees. The Cardinals were the first team to fly—hiring a mail plane to reach Chicago from Boston, where the team had been stranded by the Great Hurricane of 1938. The Dodgers flew for the first time in 1940, but wartime returned ball clubs to rail travel.

16. Ed Barrow, manager of the Red Sox from 1918 to 1920, switched Ruth from the pitching mound to the outfield in order to get his bat into the lineup every day. Barrow later became general manager of the Yankees during Ruth's heyday in the 1920s.

17. Alexander Cartwright, a New York bank teller, organized the first regular team, the Knickerbockers, and wrote the first rules governing the new sport of baseball. He set bases 90 feet apart, established nine players on a side, three outs an inning, and a fixed batting order. He developed the concept of nine innings later. The first game played under the Cartwright rules took place on June 19, 1846, at the Elysian Fields of Hoboken, New Jersey. Cartwright umpired that game to ensure that his rules were followed. The New York Nine won, 23–1. Cartwright's Cooperstown plaque credits him with being "the father of modern baseball."

18. Branch Rickey, general manager of the Cardi-

nals in 1926, came up with the farm system after he was rebuffed in trying to buy a player from the independent Joplin, Missouri, club. After Cardinal interest became known, a bidding war ensued and St. Louis was knocked out quickly. Rickey told Cardinal owner Sam Breadon, "If we can't buy the contracts of players, we'll have to raise our own." Cardinal scouts immediately began to sign large numbers of players.

19. Lou Boudreau, player-manager of the Indians, devised the Williams shift after the Red Sox slugger hit three homers, including a grand slam, to give Boston an 11–10 win in the first half of a July 14, 1946, doubleheader. In the second game, Boudreau stationed six fielders on the right side of the diamond, where the left-handed Williams placed nearly all of his hits. The leftfielder, playing deep shortstop, was the only man on the left side. Williams, refusing to sacrifice his power by hitting to the opposite field, said later that the shift—copied in modified form by other clubs—probably cost him 20–30 points off his lifetime batting average, still a more-than-respectable .344.

20. John McGraw of the New York Giants first used relief pitchers early in the century.

John McGraw spent 30 years at the helm of the New York Giants.

21.   George Moriarty.

22.   Roger Peckinpaugh was 23 when he replaced Frank Chance as manager of the New York Yankees with 17 games left in the 1914 season. Peckinpaugh later gained notoriety as the man whose eight errors at shortstop contributed to Washington's defeat by Pittsburgh, four games to three, in the 1925 World Series.

23.   Lou Boudreau of the Indians led the AL with a .327 average in 1944.

24.   Joe McCarthy finished first with the 1929 Cubs and 1932 Yankees.

Joe McCarthy found success with the Cubs and Yankees.

25.   Bill Virdon became Yankee manager in 1974, when the team played its home games in Shea Stadium, home of the Mets. He was fired before the team completed its two-year residency at Shea during the renovation of Yankee Stadium. Except for those two seasons, the Yankees have been occupants of Yankee Stadium continuously since its opening in 1923.

26.   Joe Schultz. The Pilots existed for just one year, 1969, before becoming the Milwaukee Brewers. Schultz did not accompany them. The first manager of the Brewers was Dave Bristol.

27. Coach Clyde Sukeforth, an interim manager appointed in the wake of Leo Durocher's one-year suspension for "conduct detrimental to baseball" by Commissioner A. B. (Happy) Chandler, handled the Dodgers for the first two games of the 1947 season. Though Brooklyn won both, scout Burt Shotton ran the team the rest of the way.

28. Ray Kroc, new owner of the Padres, gave his team a dressing down over the public-address system at San Diego Stadium during the 1974 home opener.

29. Sparky Anderson, three times with the Reds and once (1984) with the Tigers; and Whitey Herzog, with the 1977 Royals and 1985 Cardinals.

30. Connie Mack was 88 when he stepped down as manager of the Philadelphia Athletics after the 1950 campaign.

31. Following the 1919 Black Sox Scandal, involving alleged fixing of the World Series by members of the Chicago White Sox, baseball club owners agreed that a strong executive was needed to govern the game impartially, provide stability, and settle disputes between the leagues. Before the naming of Judge Kenesaw Mountain Landis as commissioner of baseball, league presidents acted arbitrarily in their own interests rather than in the best interests of the game. Landis ruled with a firm hand from January 12, 1921, until his death in 1944.

32. National League president John Heydler in 1928. Not until 1972, when American League attendance was falling in direct proportion to declining offense, did either league seriously consider adopting it.

33. Bucky Harris, 27, was in his fourth season as a player when he became the playing manager of the Washington Senators in 1924. He earned the "Boy Wonder" tag when his team won the pennant and the World Series. The nickname remained with him through 29 seasons as a major-league manager.

34. Player-manager Rogers Hornsby was traded from the Cardinals to the Giants after winning the 1926 World Championship for St. Louis; from the Giants, where he was strictly a player under John McGraw, to the Boston Braves, where he was again a playing manager, on January 10, 1928; and from the Braves to the Cubs, where he played two years before becoming manager, on September 23, 1930. Released by the Cubs on August 2, 1932, he signed as a player with the Cardinals, who released him on July 27, 1933, so that he could become playing manager of the St. Louis Browns. He later had another managing stint with the Browns, as well as the Reds.

35. Connie Mack of the Athletics and Burt Shotton of the Dodgers.

36. Platooning is practiced by managers who believe left-handed batters have an advantage over right-handed pitchers and right-handed hitters have an advantage over left-handed pitchers. Platooning has been a hallmark of managers dating back to George Stallings of the 1914 "miracle" Braves. Platooning at first base and two outfield positions enabled Tris Speaker's Indians to become 1920 world champions. Casey Stengel perfected the art of platooning, winning 10 pennants during his 12-year reign as manager of the Yankees from 1949 to 1960.

37. Signs are used because it is impossible for players and coaches to communicate verbally on the field. In addition to the hit or take signs, flashed by baseline coaches to players, signs order such plays as the stolen base, hit-and-run, sacrifice, and suicide squeeze. Coaches use six basic signs: bunt, take, hit-and-run, squeeze, steal, and forget-previous-sign. Defensive signs are also used, but usually with less camouflage than offensive signs.

38. Bobby Bragan, manager of the Pittsburgh Pirates, during a 1957 game.

39. Cap Anson, greatest star of the National League's first quarter century, is generally held to be the man responsible for keeping black players out of the major leagues. There were 20 black players in professional baseball in 1882—including major leaguers Fleet and Welday Walker at Toledo of the American Association. None of the blacks was made to feel welcome, and all eventually drifted out of the game.

40. During an April 1987 appearance on "Nightline," Al Campanis told ABC's Ted Koppel that blacks "lacked the necessities" to manage. The remarks caused Campanis to lose his longtime job as general manager of the Los Angeles Dodgers.

41. Preston Gomez, manager of the 1971 Padres, lifted Clay Kirby after he had hurled eight no-hit innings. He did the same thing to Don Wilson of the Astros in 1974. After he pinch hit for both men, succeeding relievers blew both games in the ninth inning. "You have to forget about personal records," Gomez said. "The name of the game is to win. If you lose, you can still feel good if you did your best."

Clay Kirby was pitching an eight-inning no-hitter for the Padres when his manager lifted him for a pinch hitter.

42. From 1961 to 1965, the Chicago Cubs operated with a rotating "college of coaches." At least a dozen head coaches were in charge at different times. The idea was the brainchild of team owner Phil Wrigley, a chewing-gum magnate who had tired of seeing his team lose in the traditional way. Ironically, the Cubs became respectable only after junking the five-year experiment and bringing Leo Durocher, a strong-willed manager with a proven track record, out of retirement.

43. After managing the Cardinals for five years, Miller Huggins became manager of the 1918 Yankees after American League president Ban Johnson initiated a meeting between Huggins and Jacob Ruppert, co-owner of the Yankees. Johnson, seeking to make the Yankees more competitive with John McGraw's powerful Giants of the National League, realized his wish when Huggins teamed with general manager Ed Barrow to piece together the original Yankee dynasty of the Babe Ruth era.

44. Branch Rickey, then running the Brooklyn Dodgers, was dubbed "the Mahatma" by writer

Tom Meany, who noted that Rickey was part paternal, part political, and part pontifical. The journalist had been reading John Gunther's *Inside Asia*, which described Mahatma Mohandas Gandhi as "an incredible combination of Jesus Christ, Tammany Hall, and your father."

45. Joe McCarthy, whose 24-year .614 winning percentage has not been matched, was called a "push-button manager" by Jimmie Dykes, who said anyone could win with the talent the Yankees had.

46. Charley Dressen of the Brooklyn Dodgers, manager of the 1953 NL All-Stars.

47. The overconfident Charley Dressen, Brooklyn manager, during the 1951 season. The Giants arose from the dead in time to win the NL pennant.

48. Billy Martin of the New York Yankees, with five.

Billy Martin managed several clubs, but none so often as the Yankees.

49. Hank Bauer.
50. Alvin Dark.

· 4 ·
TEAMS

Through most of this century, baseball has had 16 major-league teams, eight in the American League and eight in the National. Expansion gradually changed the format to the present configuration of 26 clubs (14 in the AL, 12 in the NL).

Baseball history is filled with great team performances. The New York Yankees twice won five flags in a row en route to more than 30 World Series appearances. The Dodgers, starting with the 1890 Brooklyn edition, hold the National League mark with 19 flags (17 since 1900).

While New York fans have enjoyed the successes of the Giants, Dodgers, Yankees, and Mets, Philadelphia fans have endured the unkind fate of coping with more than their share of bad ball clubs. The Phillies, with 24 cellar finishes, and the Athletics, who migrated to Kansas City and later Oakland, hold records for most times finished last. The Athletics hit rock bottom 18 times in the Quaker City and seven more times since departing for Missouri in 1955. The 1899

Cleveland Spiders of the National League still hold the all-time worst "winning percentage" of .130 (20–134).

Teams change players, managers, owners, and even cities with surprising frequency. Rooting requires loyalty through good times and bad, but team identification gives fans roots by making them feel like part of the team. Avid baseball buffs refer to their teams as "we" rather than "they," and the teams relish their unwavering support.

Teams run hot, cold, and indifferent—and often prove the axiom "Take nothing for granted in baseball."

• SCORING •

When a team gets off to a slow start, it has ample time to recover. So it is with this book. Here's how to evaluate your knowledge of teams:

52–60   Grade A. You've earned a
         championship ring.

45–51   Grade B. Definite contender.

40–44   Grade C. Respectable showing.

35–39   Grade D. Wait till next year.

Under 35 Grade F. Search for free-agent help.

• QUESTIONS •

1.   What was the original name of the Milwaukee Brewers?

2.   Name two teams that each scored a record 29 runs in a game.

3.   Who was the last active player from the original Senators?

4. Where did the team that became known as the Yankees play before moving to New York?

5. Where did the team that became known as the Browns play before moving to St. Louis?

6. What team scored 15 runs in the first inning?

7. Name the only current team with green in its uniform.

8. What team uses an elephant emblem?

9. What team had a Blue, a Green, and a Brown on its 1985 roster?

10. What team once made a 17-player trade with the Orioles?

11. What active owner once managed his team?

12. What team signed Roberto Clemente, only to lose him to Pittsburgh in the minor-league draft?

13. Name the only team to go through a season without being shut out.

14. What team had eight Hall of Famers in its lineup?

15. What team scored the most runs in an inning?

16. Name the midget who pinch hit for Bill Veeck's Browns.

17. What future Mets executive cast the lone negative vote when the directors of the New York

Giants voted 9-1 in favor of moving to San Francisco?

18. What teams played the game with the most innings?

19. Name the switch-hitting Dodger infield of 1965-66.

20. Who was the only player to play for the Braves in three cities?

21. What pitcher had the only winning record for the 1962 Mets?

22. Who was the first choice of the Mets in the NL expansion draft?

23. Who was the Cub third baseman when the rest of the infield featured the double-play combination of Tinker to Evers to Chance?

24. What two teams won the most games at the start of a season?

25. What team won 35 of its first 40 games?

26. Baseball's three top home-run hitters each started and ended his career in the same city. Name the players and the cities involved.

27. Three players from this team enjoyed four-homer games in the majors. Identify the ball club.

28. What two franchises produced a pair of 500-homer hitters?

29. What expansion team had the best debut season?

30. Name the only team to play in two different divisions.

31. The three Alou brothers came up with San Francisco but also had another team in common. Which one?

32. What team had baseball's longest undefeated streak?

33. What team had baseball's longest losing streak?

34. Name the only 20th-century team that went from 100 losses one year to a winning record the next.

35. Describe the best midseason turnaround by a ball club.

36. Why did the Phillies fail to win the 1964 pennant?

37. What pitcher got the first win in the history of the New York Mets?

38. Can groundskeepers make changes to help the home team?

39. What three teams have attracted three million fans in a season?

40. Why was the NL East once called the "National League Least"?

41. What was the "$100,000 Infield"?

42. What team has won the most pennants?

43. When did Sunday ball begin?

44. Did teams ever play tripleheaders?

45. Who holds the modern National League record for losses at the start of the season?

46. Why did the 1912 Tigers go on strike?

47. What team employed Babe Ruth when he delivered his final three-homer game?

48. What game produced the most runs?

49. Name one of the two teams to harbor four 20-game winners.

50. What team slugged the most home runs in a game?

51. The 1962 Mets had two pitchers with the same name. What was it?

52. What was the "Impossible Dream"?

53. How did "Moon shots" help the Dodgers?

54. What team built a ballpark apartment for its groundskeeper?

55. What year did a strike delay the baseball season?

56.　What team scored 1,000 runs for three straight years?

57.　Name the only city to have players sweep Triple Crown honors.

58.　Name the Minnesota city in which the Twins first played after leaving Washington.

59.　What team won 21 straight September games to clinch a pennant?

60.　Though Roger Maris achieved stardom with the Yankees, he also played for three other teams. Name them.

• ANSWERS •

1.　Seattle Pilots.

2.　The Boston Red Sox, on June 8, 1950, and the Chicago White Sox, on April 23, 1955, scored 29 runs in a game. The opponents were the St. Louis Browns and the Kansas City Athletics, respectively.

3.　Jim Kaat.

4.　Baltimore.

5.　Milwaukee.

6.　Brooklyn Dodgers, against Cincinnati, on May 21, 1952.

7.　Oakland Athletics.

8.　Oakland Athletics.

9.　San Francisco Giants.

10.　The New York Yankees, prior to the 1985 Season.

11.　Ted Turner ran the Atlanta Braves for one game in 1977 before National League president Chub

R. E. (Ted) Turner was an outspoken maverick team owner before the Bobby Cox–Chuck Tanner tandem took over baseball operations for the Atlanta Braves.

Feeney invoked Rule 20(e), which prohibits managers from having a financial interest in their team without permission from the commissioner of baseball. Turner lost the game, 2–1, to extend Atlanta's losing streak to 17 straight.

12. Brooklyn Dodgers.

13. The 1932 Yankees. The Bronx Bombers were not blanked between August 3, 1931, and August 2, 1933, a total of 308 games.

14. The 1931 New York Yankees had Babe Ruth, Lou Gehrig, Earle Combs, Bill Dickey, Herb Pennock, Lefty Gomez, Red Ruffing, and Joe Sewell.

15. On June 18, 1953, the Red Sox had a 17-run inning in the seventh against Detroit.

16. Eddie Gaedel, who stood 3'7", walked on four pitches as the Browns lost to the Tigers, 6–2, on August 19, 1951.

17. M. Donald Grant.

18. The Boston Braves and Brooklyn Dodgers played a 26-inning, 1–1 tie on May 1, 1920.

19. Wes Parker, first base; Jim Lefebvre, second base; Maury Wills, shortstop; Jim Gilliam, third base.

20.   Eddie Mathews.

Longtime Braves' star Eddie Mathews is the only man to play for, coach, and manage the club.

21.   Ken MacKenzie was 5–4 for a team that lost 120 games.

22.   San Francisco catcher Hobie Landrith.

23.   Harry Steinfeldt, who hit .327 to help the Cubs win a major-league record 116 games in 1906. Chicago won four pennants in his first five seasons.

24.   The 1982 Atlanta Braves and 1987 Milwaukee Brewers both rocketed to 13–0 starts.

25.   The 1984 Tigers.

26.   Hank Aaron, Milwaukee; Babe Ruth, Boston; Willie Mays, New York.

27.   Philadelphia Phillies (Ed Delahanty, Chuck Klein, Mike Schmidt).

28.   New York Yankees (Babe Ruth, Mickey Mantle) and the New York–San Francisco Giants (Mel Ott, Willie Mays).

29.   The Los Angeles (now California) Angels finished eighth in a 10-team league with a 70–91 record in 1961, their first season. The very next year, however, they moved up to third, 10 games from the top, with an 86–76 log.

30. Milwaukee Brewers. Created as the Seattle Pilots in 1969, the Brewers remained in the AL West until the Washington Senators of the AL East became the Texas Rangers in 1972. The league placed Texas in the West and shifted Milwaukee to the East.

31. Oakland Athletics.

32. The 1916 New York Giants won 26 straight (with one tie), giving them an undefeated streak of 27 games.

33. The 1961 Phillies lost a modern-record 23 in a row.

34. The 1986 Giants.

35. On August 11, 1951, the New York Giants trailed the Brooklyn Dodgers by 13 games but came back to go 39–8 down the stretch, tying for first place and then winning the best-of-three pennant playoff on Bobby Thomson's three-run homer in the last inning of the last game.

36. Leading the Cardinals by six-and-a-half games with 12 games to play, the Phils overworked their top starting pitchers, lost 10 straight, and finished in a second-place tie with Cincinnati, one game behind St. Louis.

37. Jay Hook, a mechanical engineer who could explain the mechanics of a curveball more easily than he could throw one, got the first Met win after the team made its 1962 bow with nine consecutive losses.

38. Yes. Groundskeepers can make legal changes to help home teams win. They can water the base paths or slope the foul lines to thwart bunt-and-steal teams, let the grass grow long to compensate for a slow-footed third baseman, or take extra time in placing or replacing the tar-

paulin during rain delays. Groundskeepers pay special attention to the batter's box, pitcher's mound, and baselines. Pitchers have their own preferences about the height and texture of the dirt on the mound. Connie Mack, for example, kept his mound 20 inches high for ace pitchers Lefty Grove, George Earnshaw, Chief Bender, and Eddie Plank, even though the average height is about 10 inches.

When Ty Cobb played for Detroit, opposing teams kept their infield grass short to cause his bunts and infield rollers to reach infielders more quickly. Years later, the Indians let their grass grow long to make life easier for third baseman Al Rosen.

Cardinal manager Eddie Stanky was among those incensed at the Phillies for keeping the third-base line inclined slightly to keep Richie Ashburn's bunts from rolling foul. Stanky's attack on "Ashburn's Ridge" included a regular pre-game routine of scraping away the infield dirt with his spikes.

39.   The St. Louis Cardinals, Los Angeles Dodgers, and New York Mets.

40.   With six days to go in the 1973 season, five of the six teams in the NL East still had a chance to finish first, with a remote chance that a five-way deadlock—all teams at 80–82—could develop. The Mets eventually prevailed with an 82–79 record, for a .509 winning percentage, the lowest ever recorded by a championship team. When the Mets upset the favored Cincinnati Reds in the Championship Series, critics charged that the NL's World Series entry represented the "National League Least."

41.   The 1911 Philadelphia Athletics featured base-

ball's best infield: John (Stuffy) McInnis at first, Eddie Collins at second, Jack Barry at shortstop, and Frank (Home Run) Baker at third. The quartet was known as the "$100,000 Infield" because Connie Mack could have acquired that sum—an enormous amount of money in those days—in exchange for his star infielders.

42. The Yankees have won a record 33 through 1982.

43. During its first two seasons, 1876–77, the National League threatened to expel teams and players for playing on Sunday. The NL finally recognized Sunday ball by 1892, even though municipal blue laws prohibited many teams from scheduling Sunday games. Sunday ball came to New York in 1917 but was not universally accepted in the majors until the mid-thirties.

44. Yes. Tripleheaders have been played several times, most recently in 1920. During the last week of the 1920 season, the fourth-place Pirates had a chance to catch the third-place Reds and earn a slice of the World Series money pool (divided among the top three finishers during the 154-game format). Cincinnati was scheduled to play three games against Pittsburgh before both clubs finished the season with single games against other opponents. Four Pirate wins coupled with four Red losses would have given Pittsburgh third place, but a Friday rainout dampened Pirate hopes. Resourceful Pirate owner Barney Dreyfuss then suggested that the Saturday doubleheader be changed to a tripleheader. Cincinnati manager Pat Moran refused, but Dreyfuss got NL president John Heydler to overrule him—an easy decision since there was baseball precedent (in 1890 Pitts-

burgh swept Brooklyn in a tripleheader, and six years later Baltimore swept Louisville). Unfortunately for Dreyfuss, the Reds won the first two games to clinch third place. The third game was shortened to six innings because of darkness.

45. The 1988 Atlanta Braves lost 10 straight to open the season.

46. On May 15, 1912, Detroit superstar Ty Cobb was suspended indefinitely by the American League for jumping into the stands to attack a heckler in New York. Cobb's teammates wired the league office that they would strike until he was reinstated. On May 18, when Cobb took the field with his teammates in Philadelphia, the umpires ordered him off. The rest of the team went with him. Manager Hugh Jennings, who came prepared, immediately activated two coaches and recruited some semipros, including a future priest named Al Travers, who pitched the entire game, to play the Athletics. Detroit lost, 24–2. The American League ordered the striking Tigers back, threatening them with lifetime expulsion if they didn't return, and fined them $100 each. Cobb was reinstated on May 25 and ordered to pay a $50 fine.

47. Boston Braves, May 25, 1935.

48. Cubs 26, Phillies 23, for a total of 49 runs, on August 24, 1922.

49. The 1920 White Sox and 1971 Orioles.

50. The Blue Jays hit 10 during an 18–3 win over Baltimore on September 14, 1987.

51. Bob Miller. Bob G. Miller was left-handed and Bob L. Miller was right-handed.

52. The Red Sox overcame 100-to-1 odds to win the 1967 American League flag in a photo finish

over the Tigers and Twins, both one game out at season's end, and the White Sox, who were three games out.

Going into the final weekend, Minnesota led Boston and Detroit by one game. But Boston beat Minnesota twice at Fenway Park, then awaited the outcome of the season-ending doubleheader between Detroit and California. A Detroit sweep would have forced a playoff, but California won the second game to give Boston the pennant. The last weekend victory by the Bosox capped a rags-to-riches season in which the young Boston team, powered by Triple Crown winner Carl Yastrzemski, rose from ninth place (in a 10-team league) in 1966 to first in 1967. Writers called the comeback the "Impossible Dream," taking the title from the featured song in the popular Broadway show *Man of La Mancha*.

53. During their first four years in California, the Los Angeles Dodgers played in the Los Angeles Coliseum, a converted football field, while waiting for Dodger Stadium to be built. The left-field wall, 250 feet from home plate, proved a boon to right-handed batters even though it had a 42-foot-high fence attached to make it seem like a legitimate major-league configuration. With the right-center-field power alley 440 feet away, life was difficult for Duke Snider and other left-handed hitters—with the sole exception of Wally Moon. In the first 10 games of the 1961 season, Moon—who could hit to the opposite field—golfed six balls over the screen, prompting writers to dub his blasts "Moon shots" after that year's first manned American space capsule. Moon finished the year with 17 home runs.

54.   During the 1930s, New York Giants' owner Horace Stoneham enticed Marty Schwab, head groundskeeper of the Brooklyn Dodgers, to work for the Giants by building an apartment for the Schwab family inside the Polo Grounds. The Schwabs, who lived under Section 31 in left field, remain the only groundskeeping family to have lived and worked in the same place.

55.   1972.

56.   The Yankees of 1930–32. The only other teams to score that many runs in a season were the 1930 Cardinals, 1936 Yankees, and the 1950 Red Sox.

57.   Philadelphia in 1933. Jimmie Foxx of the Athletics won the American League's Triple Crown, while Chuck Klein of the Phillies won in the National.

58.   Bloomington.

59.   The 1935 Cubs.

60.   Cleveland Indians, Kansas City Athletics, and St. Louis Cardinals.

• 5 •

BALLPARKS

Because no two ballparks are alike, baseball will always fuel great debates. Not only do weather conditions vary from site to site, but park dimensions—often dictated by available real estate when fields were built—are decidely different.

Early parks were made of wood and had limited seating capacity. Often, there were no outfield fences and only a rope barrier (to ward off gate-crashers). Horse-drawn carriages—succeeded by horseless carriages—parked deep in the outfield after entering through special gates.

On days when spectator turnout exceeded expectations, fans stood behind roped-off sections of outfield—creating the need for special ground rules to govern balls hit into the crowd.

Because of their wood construction, a number of parks were consumed by fire. Concrete-and-steel stadiums began to spring up early in this century. Sportsman's Park in St. Louis was first used during the National League's inaugural 1876 season and remained in continuous use until May 8, 1966 (except for the period 1878–1884, when the city had no team). Reinforcement with concrete and steel in 1908 was the reason for the park's longevity.

Like players, owners, and managers, ballparks have personalities. Batted balls carry well in Atlanta and Philadelphia, but the current home of the Cardinals, Busch Stadium, is a graveyard for home-run hitters. Right-handed hitters feast at Boston's Fenway Park, while lefties relish Yankee Stadium, Tiger Stadium, and Minnesota's Hubert H. Humphrey Metrodome.

The advent of covered ballparks precluded postponements and introduced an element that changed the game dramatically: artificial turf. Like the game itself, stadiums have come a long way since 1876.

• SCORING •

Television has brought dozens of different ballparks into living rooms across America. How well do you know them? Use this scoring chart:

35–40	Grade A. Your baseball brain is operating at full capacity.
30–34	Grade B. A slow grounds crew keeps your park from perfection.
25–29	Grade C. It's time to refurbish the old ball yard.
20–24	Grade D. Stadium condemned.
Under 20	Grade F. Nothing will fill your park.

• QUESTIONS •

1. Before moving to California, the Brooklyn Dodgers played 15 home games in another ballpark. Name it.

2. Name the last park to be illuminated for night baseball.

3. What was the site of the first major-league baseball game on the West Coast?

4. Name three domed parks that have hosted All-Star Games.

5. Why do ballparks have dirt or gravel tracks around the outfield?

6. What was the first indoor major-league stadium?

7. Where did the Mets play before Shea Stadium opened?

8. Where did the Phillies play before the 1971 opening of Veterans Stadium?

9. What is the oldest active park?

10. What is the smallest active ball park?

11. Why is Yankee Stadium called "The House That Ruth Built"?

12. Why is Fenway Park a graveyard for pitchers?

13. How did their home parks hurt Ted Williams and Joe DiMaggio?

A jam of jalopies added to the chaos at the opening of Yankee Stadium in 1923. Some 75,000 fans jammed the new ballpark, while another 25,000 were turned away at the gates.

14. Why was New York's Polo Grounds the toughest and easiest home-run target?

15. What three hitters hit balls into the center-field bleachers at the Polo Grounds?

16. What ballpark was once called the "Launching Pad"?

17. What pitcher won the last game at Ebbets Field?

18. Who hit the last Polo Grounds home run?

19. What is the "Green Monster"?

20. Name the only Dodger to hit two home runs in Jersey City's Roosevelt Stadium.

21. Why don't all ballparks have the same configurations?

22. Name the only active NL park that was never the site of a no-hitter.

23. What Pirate pitched a no-hitter at Forbes Field?

24. Why is Minnesota's stadium nicknamed the "Homerdome"?

25. What is the "goat curse of Wrigley Field"?

26. Who hit the first home run in the Astrodome?

27. What current stadium has the largest seating capacity?

28. Name the ballpark where 93,000 fans attended a major-league game.

29. Where did Hank Aaron hit the home run that tied Babe Ruth's record?

30. Where did an outfield advertisement encourage batters to "HIT SIGN, WIN SUIT"?

31. What was the original name of Connie Mack Stadium?

32. What stadium hosted both the Browns and Cardinals?

33. What former NL park was reassembled by a farmer?

34. Where did the Seattle Pilots play?

35. What was the first home of the California Angels?

36. What park was the home of the original Washington Senators?

37. Before its name was changed to Robert F. Kennedy Stadium, what was the name of the second-edition Senators' home park?

38. Wind is often a significant factor in these two active parks. Name them.

39. Where was "Greenberg Gardens" located?

40. What stadium contained a "pennant porch"?

• ANSWERS •

1. Roosevelt Stadium, Jersey City, hosted the Dodgers for seven "home" games in 1956 and another seven in 1957.

2. Wrigley Field, Chicago, finally turned on the lights on August 8, 1988, the Phillies vs. the Cubs. The game was rained out, making the August 9 game against the Mets the first official night game at Wrigley.

3. Seals Stadium, San Francisco. The Giants blanked the Dodgers, 8–0, on April 15, 1958, before a capacity crowd of 22,900.

4. Houston Astrodome, Seattle Kingdome, and Hubert H. Humphrey Metrodome (Minnesota).

5. Warning tracks tell outfielders they are about to encounter barriers. Teams made no effort to ensure outfielder safety until Pete Reiser of the Dodgers was seriously hurt crashing into the Ebbets Field wall in 1947. Reiser, hurt previously the same way in St. Louis, was out of action long enough to convince the Dodgers that walls should be padded. Soon after they added the padding, narrow cinder "warning tracks" appeared in Wrigley Field, Chicago; Shibe Park, Philadelphia; and Braves Field, Boston. Today all major-league stadiums feature dirt warning tracks to alert outfielders they are nearing the walls.

6. The Houston Astrodome, opened in 1965.

7. The Polo Grounds, former home of the New York Giants.

8. Connie Mack Stadium, formerly known as Shibe Park.

9. Chicago's Comiskey, home of the White Sox, opened in 1910.

10. Boston's Fenway Park holds 33,000 fans.

11. After Babe Ruth became a member of the Yankees in 1920, fans turned out for Yankee games in record numbers. The 1920 Yankees drew 1,289,422, then a major-league record. The landlord New York Giants told them to find a new home. Col. Jacob Ruppert, co-owner of the Yankees, bought a Bronx lumberyard across the Harlem River from the Polo Grounds and built Yankee Stadium with the proceeds produced by Ruth's appeal as a gate attraction. When Yankee Stadium opened on April 18, 1923, the crowd inside the park was announced as 74,217, although it was probably even larger. Thousands more were turned away. Ruth's three-

run homer made the difference in New York's 4–1 win over the Red Sox.

12. Cozy dimensions, particularly the distance from home plate to left field, make Fenway Park a hitters' paradise. The left-field wall stands 315 feet from home plate, making high-scoring games common. In 1950 the Red Sox took consecutive 20–4 and 29–4 games from the St. Louis Browns.

13. Right-handed hitter Joe DiMaggio played half his games in Yankee Stadium, an easy home-run target for left-handed hitters, while left-handed hitter Ted Williams played half his games in Boston's Fenway Park, an easy home-run target for right-handed hitters. A DiMaggio-Williams trade, which nearly happened in 1949, might have allowed both men to challenge single-season and career home-run records. Williams managed 521 career homers anyway in a career twice interrupted by military service. DiMaggio finished his career with 361.

14. Dimensions at the Polo Grounds were 279 feet down the left-field line, 254 feet to the right-field corner, but 483 feet to the inset center-field clubhouses. Long drives, if not hit down the lines, were often noisy outs at the Polo Grounds.

15. Joe Adcock, Hank Aaron, and Lou Brock. Adcock did it on April 29, 1953; Brock on June 17, 1962; and Aaron connected with the bases loaded the following night, on June 18, 1962.

16. Atlanta-Fulton County Stadium earned the name in 1966, when Pat Jarvis, then the ace pitcher of the Braves, told newly arrived hurlers, "There it is, boys. Welcome to the Launching Pad. The ball really jumps out of here." Atlanta's altitude—1,050 feet above sea level (highest in

the majors)—is a contributing factor to the high home-run totals at the ballpark. The cozy dimensions—330 feet down the lines—also help.

Balls often rocket out of Atlanta–Fulton County Stadium.

17.   Danny McDevitt of the Dodgers beat Pittsburgh, 2–0, on September 24, 1957.

18.   Jim Hickman of the Mets, against Philadelphia, on September 18, 1963.

19.   The left-field wall at Boston's Fenway Park. It was named by pitchers both for its color and its impact on their earned-run average.

20.   Duke Snider.

21.   The first ballparks were erected within city limits so that fans could get there on local streetcar lines. The shape of these parks was usually dictated by existing streets and buildings. It is for this reason that such older parks as Wrigley Field (Cubs) and Fenway Park (Red Sox) seem so confined. Wrigley has little foul territory, while

Fenway features a left-field wall most pitchers feel is too close to home plate. More recent ballparks, built in suburbia, are more spacious and have more uniforn dimensions.

22. Veterans Stadium, Philadelphia.

23. No one. Nick Maddox pitched one in Pittsburgh in 1907, before Forbes Field opened, and Pirate John Candelaria pitched one at Three Rivers Stadium, successor to Forbes Field in the Steel City. Forbes Field was in use from 1909 to 1970.

24. When the Minnesota Twins began playing in the 54,000-seat Hubert H. Humphrey Metrodome in 1982, they quickly discovered that the air jets used to keep the roof inflated provided atmospheric conditions conducive to the long ball. The short right field—327 feet down the line—also helped. With balls flying over the Metrodome fences in record numbers, writers dubbed the park the "Homerdome."

The Hubert H. Humphrey Metrodome, home of the Twins, was known as a home-run haven long before the 1987 World Series.

25. During the 1945 season, a fan brought his pet goat to every game at Wrigley Field. But the animal was barred during the World Series, so

angering its owner that he placed a hex on the club. The Cubs would never make the World Series again, he said. Through the 1987 season, the curse has held.

26. Mickey Mantle hit the first one, in an exhibition game on April 9, 1965. Three days later, Dick Allen of the Phillies hit the first official Astrodome homer.

27. Cleveland's Municipal Stadium holds 77,797.

28. The Dodgers drew 92,706 fans to a 1959 World Series game against the White Sox in the Los Angeles Coliseum. The largest crowd ever to watch a baseball game—93,103—saw the Dodger-Yankee exhibition game on May 7, 1959, Roy Campanella Night at the Coliseum. The regular-season record is owned by the Cleveland Indians, who drew 84,597 to a doubleheader against the Yankees on September 12, 1954.

29. Cincinnati's Riverfront Stadium, on April 4, 1974.

30. Ebbets Field, Brooklyn.

31. Shibe Park.

32. Sportsman's Park, St. Louis.

33. Crosley Field, onetime home of the Reds, was rebuilt in Blue Ash, Ohio, as a tourist attraction. It was rededicated in 1988.

34. Sicks Stadium.

35. The team, then called the Los Angeles Angels, played one year in Wrigley Field, a former minor-league park, before becoming tenants at Dodger Stadium. Anaheim Stadium opened in 1966.

36. Griffith Stadium.

37. D.C. Stadium.

38. Candlestick Park (San Francisco) and Wrigley Field (Chicago).

39. Forbes Field in Pittsburgh, where Hank Greenburg spent his final season in 1947, contained Greenberg Gardens, an enclosure that reduced the distance to left field from 365 to 335 feet and cut the distance from home plate to left-center by 20 feet. The area was renamed Kiner's Korner when Ralph Kiner succeeded Greenberg as the top Pittsburgh slugger.

40. Municipal Stadium in Kansas City, the onetime home of the Athletics, was the site where owner Charles O. Finley attempted to build a "Pennant Porch" in the mid-sixties. Finley had hoped to restructure his right-field dimensions to match those of Yankee Stadium, but commisioner of baseball Ford Frick and AL president Joe Cronin ordered it dismantled after two exhibition games. The executives ruled that the "Pennant Porch" violated a league rule that the distance from home plate to any outfield fence could not be less than 325 feet. The rule, passed on June 1, 1958, said remodeling of existing parks could not include shortening of distances to fences below the 325-foot standard. Finley had sought to duplicate the old 296-foot distance from home plate to the right-field foul pole at Yankee Stadium.

· 6 ·
RULES AND EQUIPMENT

Baseball is a game that is easy for the casual fan to understand, but complex enough to provide ample ammunition for the second-guesser. It is a game played by rules that have evolved over more than a century of trial and error. And it is a game governed by officials whose knowledge of those rules must be tempered with shrewd interpretation, personal judgment, and ironclad consistency.

To some observers, baseball seems simple: nine men on a side, nine innings, a diamond-shaped infield cornered by three bases and home plate, three outs an inning, and limits of four balls and three strikes on each batter. But former National League umpire Paul Pryor insists the game is much more intricate than that.

"Most fans go out to the ballpark to enjoy themselves," he says, "but I bet they don't know one rule out of 20. When clubs sell season tickets, they should give the fans rule books so they can follow the game more closely."

Game rules are enforced by umpires, the policemen of the sport.

"You're only as good as your last call," umpire Bill Haller once said. "You can call 100 in a row right but miss that last one, and that's the one they'll remember."

• SCORING •

How much do you know about baseball rules and its enforcers? Chart your expertise as follows:

18–20	Grade A. Rivals never question your judgment.
15–17	Grade B. A tough opponent in an argument.
12–14	Grade C. You missed a few close calls.
10–11	Grade D. Stuck at the Triple A level.
Under 10	Flunked umpire school.

• QUESTIONS •

1. As chief enforcer of the rules, he was such a good umpire that he was assigned exclusive duty behind the plate for his first 16 seasons. Name him.

2. Why was Hank Aaron once declared out after hitting a home run?

3. What was "Merkle's boner"?

4. Whose ninth-inning homer triggered a controversial pine-tar protest?

5. Why did baseball institute the foul-strike rule?

6. Is there a rule limiting the size of gloves worn by catchers and first basemen?

7. Why do catchers wear so much equipment?

8. What is a Louisville Slugger?

9. How did Babe Ruth influence bat making?

10. Does the curveball actually curve?

11. What is the phantom double play?

12. When did batters start wearing helmets?

13. How did an appeal play save a no-hitter?

14. Does a no-hitter count if rain shortens the game?

15. Why do umpires use exaggerated hand signals?

16. What batter, hit by a Don Drysdale pitch with the bases loaded, was not allowed to take first base?

17. What is a balk?

18. How has pitching distance changed over the years?

19. How many warm-up throws can a relief pitcher take?

20. Why did baseball ban the spitball?

• ANSWERS •

1. Hall of Famer Bill Klem.

2. On August 18, 1965, Hank Aaron's shot onto the roof of Sportsman's Park in St. Louis was ruled an out by umpire Chris Pelekoudas. The arbiter made the call when Cardinal catcher Bob Uecker pointed out that Aaron's back foot had been out of the batter's box. The rules dictate that the batter must remain in the box until the pitcher delivers the ball, but that the umpire is not obliged to cite the infraction unless the opposing team appeals.

3. On September 24, 1908, the New York Giants and Chicago Cubs were tied 1–1 in the bottom of the ninth at the Polo Grounds. With Moose McCormick on third and Fred Merkle at first with two outs, Al Bridwell singled to center. Though McCormick scored the apparent winning run, Merkle stopped short of second and headed for the clubhouse. The Cubs alertly appealed and attempted to throw to second for the force play that would have nullified the run. New York pitcher Joe (Iron Man) McGinnity, realizing their intent, seized the ball and hurled it into the crowd, but umpire Hank O'Day charged him with interference and ruled Merkle out. The fans swarming over the field did not realize the game had ended in a 1–1 tie. At season's end, the Giants and Cubs had identical 98–55 records and had to replay the game that ended with Merkle's boner. Chicago won the replay and the pennant. In addition, Merkle's blunder cost Christy Mathewson the victory that would have placed him third on the career victory list by himself. Instead, he shares that honor with Grover Cleveland Alexander (both had 373 wins).

4. George Brett of the Royals hit a two-run, ninth-inning homer against the Yankees on July 24, 1983, but umpires ruled it a game-ending out after New York manager Billy Martin lodged a protest on the basis of Brett's bat. The umpires determined that the pine tar on Brett's bat exceeded the legal limit. Though Rule 6.06(d) stipulates that any batter using an altered bat to improve distance must be ruled out, American League president Lee MacPhail overruled his umpires and said the game should be resumed from the point of the home run. Kansas City eventually won by the 5-4 score. MacPhail, who had never upheld a protest in 10 previous years as AL chief executive, said he had determined that Brett's intent was to use the pine tar not to improve distance but to get a better grip on the bat.

5. Before the turn of the century, when foul balls were not counted as strikes, clever hitters wore out rival pitchers by deliberately hitting pitches foul until they found serves they liked. Nor were foul bunts on the third strike considered strikeouts. In 1901 the Phillies' leadoff hitter, Roy Thomas, proved so adept at causing delays by hitting fouls that the rule makers decided to count all fouls as strikes except in third-strike situations. Nevertheless, many early-century players continued the practice of hitting deliberate fouls. One player who proved a master of the practice was Luke Appling, who played from 1930 to 1950.

6. Catchers and first basemen handle more throws—and have to hang onto more wild throws—than any other players. Though rivals ridiculed Hank Greenberg for wearing a big, fishnet-style mitt in the 1930s, he was able to

reach and hold balls other first basemen missed. Baseball then passed a rule limiting the size of the first baseman's mitt to 8 inches across and 12 inches in length. Years later, similar restrictive legislation was passed for catchers' mitts after Baltimore Oriole manager Paul Richards devised a huge glove so that catcher Gus Triandos could hold onto Hoyt Wilhelm's knuckleball. Current rules allow catchers' mitts to be no more than 38 inches in circumference, nor more than 15½ inches from top to bottom.

7. Without adequate protection, catchers would often be hurt by wild pitches, thrown bats, and foul tips, as well as by trick pitches that are often as hard to catch as they are to hit. Harvard coach Fred Thayer devised the first catcher's mask in 1875, but a tinsmith replaced the mesh face with wide-spaced iron bars. In 1885 catchers and umpires began wearing primitive chest protectors. The first padded catcher's mitt, devised by Buck Ewing of the New York Giants, appeared five years later. Another Giant, catcher Roger Bresnahan, wore the first shin guards in 1908.

8. The name "Louisville Slugger" stems from a nineteenth-century bat order placed by Pete Browning, star slugger for a Louisville team called "The Eclipse." The day after 18-year-old Bud Hillerich turned the bat for Browning, the slugger went 3 for 3. Word spread and the simple wood-turning shop of J. F. Hillerich became a bat-making plant. The Hillerich & Bradsby Company has since moved to Jeffersonville, Indiana, some eight miles from Louisville.

9. Before the 1919 season, Babe Ruth told Hillerich & Bradsby to make him a bat with a narrow

handle and a knob—the first time that style had been ordered. The R43 model used by Ruth that year produced 29 homers, best in the majors, and sparked a flurry of interest from other players, revolutionizing the bat-making industry. Hillerich & Bradsby, which celebrated its 100th anniversary in 1984, now makes 20,000 Louisville Sluggers, all made-to-order, for major-league players each season.

10. A study in aerodynamics, the curveball can actually curve up to 17½ inches from its initial path, according to the National Bureau of Standards. When the ball is gripped with the thumb touching the seam at the bottom and the second finger and the third finger on top, the rotation of the thrown ball will catch air currents and cause the ball to arc across the plate. Candy Cummings threw the first curveball in 1864.

11. The pivotman—either the second baseman or shortstop—does not actually step on second as he takes the throw before throwing to first. If he does step on the bag, he may not have the ball in his possession at the precise moment his foot is on the base. Umpires will credit the phantom force-out at second if the attempt is reasonably close—primarily because they realize the pivotman must leap to avoid the oncoming baserunner.

12. The A. J. Reach Company invented the Reach Pneumatic Batters' Head Protector in 1907 after Roger Bresnahan was knocked unconscious by a pitch. The Giants' catcher became the first player to wear this forerunner of the modern helmet, though contemporaries wore "protective" inserts inside their caps. It wasn't until 1950 that Cleveland engineers Ed Crick and Ralph

Davis invented modern fiberglass and resin helmets. Seven years later, the wearing of helmets was mandated by the American League.

13.   Near the end of the 1923 season, Red Sox pitcher Howard Ehmke lost his no-hitter against the Philadelphia Athletics when rival pitcher Slim Harriss hit an apparent double off the right-field fence. But Harriss failed to touch first and was ruled out when the Red Sox appealed, saving Ehmke's no-hitter.

14.   Yes. Mike McCormick of the Giants got credit for an abbreviated no-hitter on June 12, 1959— even though he yielded an infield hit to Richie Ashburn in the sixth. When rain washed out the top of the sixth, the score reverted back to the previous full inning and McCormick was credited with a fluke no-hitter. Four other pitchers received credit for abbreviated no-hitters when games were halted to allow teams to catch trains. The ultimate shortened no-hitter occurred on October 5, 1907, when Rube Vickers of the Philadelphia Athletics pitched 12 innings of four-hit relief in a doubleheader opener, then started the nightcap and pitched five perfect innings before darkness halted play.

15.   The practice of using hand signals for strikes started around the turn of the century, when a deaf-mute named William (Dummy) Hoy asked the home plate umpire to raise his hand to signify a strike. Hand signals also enable the scorer, the media, and the spectators to keep up-to-date in the ball-and-strike count on the batter. Umpire Bill Klem began to use exaggerated gestures for strike calls in 1905, three years after Hoy left the majors.

16. Dick Dietz of the Giants was nicked by a Drysdale pitch with the bases loaded in the ninth inning of a Dodger-Giant game on May 31, 1968. But umpire Harry Wendelstedt cited Rule 6.08b(2), which prohibits a batter from taking a base if he makes no attempt to avoid the pitched ball. The fact that Drysdale had pitched 44 consecutive scoreless innings, 12 short of Walter Johnson's record, may have influenced Wendelstedt's thinking. After hitting two fouls on the 3-2 count, Dietz hit a short fly to left—not deep enough to score a run—for the first out. Ty Cline grounded into a force at home and Jack Hiatt popped to first, giving Drysdale a 3-0 win and keeping his streak alive. He eventually passed Johnson, working 58-2/3 consecutive scoreless frames before yielding a run.

17. A balk is an illegal motion by a pitcher working with men on base. When it is called by an umpire, baserunners can advance one base. Among the reasons for a balk call is an attempt by a pitcher to throw to a base without first stepping toward that base, or an attempt by a pitcher to deliver a pitch without coming to a complete stop in the set position.

18. The pitching distance was originally 45 feet from mound to home plate. That changed to 50 feet in 1881, then the current distance of 60 feet, 6 inches—because the surveyor misread the *0* inches as a *6*—in 1893. Until 1881, pitchers had to throw underhand and faced numerous other restrictions that distorted early records. Batters were also able to "order" the kind of pitches they wanted.

19. Eight.

20. The 1920 ban on the spitball was part of a

sweeping reform effort to clean up baseball in the wake of the Black Sox Scandal. The spitball, which sinks sharply as it nears home plate, contributed to the lack of offense in the first part of the century; it was eliminated to give batters more opportunities. Baseball ownership had decided that the best defense from the Black Sox black eye was a good offense on the field. Seventeen known spitballers in 1920 were permitted to continue using the pitch.

• 7 •

OCTOBER MADNESS

Though some players insist the League Championship Series, a product of divisional play, has super-
seded the World Series in significance, most baseball
insiders contend that the best-of-seven competition
between league champions retains its traditional role
as the highlight of the baseball year.

With few exceptions—caused by quirks in the
preceding playoffs—the World Series stands as a test
of skills between baseball's best teams. Games are
played under the glare of the public spotlight, but
teams emerging from tight pennant races sometimes
tend to let down in the Fall Classic.

Series history is filled with high drama and bitter
disappointment. Babe Ruth starred as both pitcher
and hitter in World Series play but rode the Series
bench during his rookie year and wore goat's horns
for a stupid play 11 years later, at a time when he was
the game's brightest star.

Ralph Terry of the Yankees yielded the last-game,
last-inning homer that lost the 1960 World Series to the

Pirates but survived another Game 7 scare two years later when he escaped with a 1-0 victory over the Giants.

World Series excitement has included a perfect game and a near no-hitter, several three-homer games, daredevil baserunning, untimely errors, and a list of heroics too lengthy to duplicate here.

The League Championship Series, created in 1969, began as a best-of-five competition between winners from the East and West, then was expanded to the best-of-seven format in 1985. Intradivisional ties are settled the same way season-ending ties were broken in the past—clubs with identical records clashed for the right to advance to the next level of competition. All of it is part of October Madness.

• SCORING •

When the regular baseball season ends, the season is just beginning for many fans. Use the following chart to determine your knowledge of postseason activity:

65–75	Grade A. Happy Halloween! Wear your baseball uniform proudly.
55–64	Grade B. Like the 1984 Cubs, close but no cigar.
45–54	Grade C. Your team ties for first, folds in the playoffs.
40–44	Grade D. Take your pick: '64 Phillies or '87 Blue Jays.
Under 40	Grade F. Hide your head in a pumpkin.

• QUESTIONS •

1. How many World Series games did Bob Feller win?

2. Name the rookie reliever who had two wins and two saves for the Dodgers in the 1959 World Series.

3. Name the only pitcher to work all seven games of a World Series.

4. How did Babe Ruth make the last out of the 1926 World Series?

5. Name the two players who had three-homer World Series games.

6. Who was on deck when Bobby Thomson's three-run, ninth-inning homer gave the 1951 New York Giants a 5–4 victory and the NL flag?

After hitting the most dramatic home run in baseball history, Bobby Thomson is hugged by Horace Stoneham (left), owner of the New York Giants, and manager Leo Durocher.

7. What Dodger hit two pinch homers in the 1959 World Series?

8. Name the only other player to hit two pinch homers in a Series.

9. What future Yankee manager hit two game-winning homers against the Yankees in one World Series?

10. Who hit the only sudden-death home run to decide a World Series?

11. Who had a three-homer game in the American League Championship Series?

12. What pitcher hit a grand slam in the ALCS?

13. What best-of-five Championship Series was decided by a ninth-inning home run?

14. Who fanned a record 17 hitters in a World Series opener?

15. Who was the losing pitcher in Don Larsen's perfect game?

16. Whose unexpected homer helped the Yankees beat the Red Sox in the only one-game playoff to decide the American League East title?

17. What pinch hitter helped the 1954 New York Giants sweep the favored Cleveland Indians in the World Series?

18. Name two pitchers who fanned 14 hitters in ALCS games.

19. What teams—one in each league—overcame 2-0 deficits to win best-of-five Championship Series?

20. Whose 12th-inning homer sent the 1975 World Series into Game 7?

21. What team scored 10 runs in a World Series inning?

22. Whose mad dash won the 1946 World Series for St. Louis?

23. Name the only pitcher to hit a World Series grand slam.

24. Name at least three teams that have rebounded from a 3-1 game deficit in the World Series.

25. What year was the first all-Astroturf World Series?

26. Name three 1947 World Series heroes who failed to remain in the major leagues in 1948.

27. Who was the victim of Babe Ruth's 1932 ``called shot'' homer?

Controversy continues over the Babe Ruth gesture, captured by artist Robert Thom, that marked the 1932 Yankee-Cub World Series. The gesture occurred in the fifth inning of a 4-4 game, with the count 2-and-2. Ruth hit the next pitch for his second home run of the day.

28. Whose "snooze" at the plate cost his team a World Series game?

29. Whose ninth-inning passed ball helped the Yankees win a World Series?

30. What was the "$30,000 Muff"?

31. Who yielded Bill Mazeroski's Series-winning homer?

32. Name the only brothers to homer in the same World Series game.

33. Who pitched three World Series shutouts in six days?

34. Name the only World Series pitcher who did not bat last.

35. How many players have homered in the All-Star Game, League Championship Series, and World Series in the same season?

36. Who hit the first grand slam for the National League in a World Series?

37. Identify the two players—one on each team—who appeared in both the 1951 and 1962 Dodger-Giant pennant playoffs.

38. Name the only man to play in every World Series game between the Brooklyn Dodgers and New York Yankees.

39. Who hit the first pinch homer in a World Series?

40. Who was the National League's first designated hitter?

41. Who hit the first World Series grand slam?

42. Who hit the most World Series home runs?

43. Who holds the NL record for World Series home runs?

44. Name the only player with a World Series home run who never hit one during regular-season play.

45. Identify the only player with a pair of two-homer games in a World Series.

Dick Williams was managing the Oakland Athletics when he got fed up with the antics of his owner during a World Series.

46. Which was the first team to sweep a World Series?

47. What player's "firing" during a World Series caused a manager to quit?

48. Name the lone National Leaguer to hit three home runs in a Championship Series game.

49. Who was the last player-manager in a World Series?

50. Name the only man to hit three homers in a postseason game that his team lost.

51. Why did Vince Coleman of the Cardinals miss the 1985 World Series?

52. Whose error allowed the Mets to win Game 6 of the 1986 Series?

53. Whose two-out, two-strike, ninth-inning homer kept the Red Sox from elimination during the 1986 ALCS?

54. What switch hitter went eight years without a left-handed home run before hitting one in a postseason game?

55. Who has appeared in the most postseason games?

56. Whose 10th-inning homer broke up a scoreless ALCS game that clinched a pennant?

57. Whose wild pitch gave the Reds a pennant?

58. Who holds the record for RBI in a World Series?

59. Identify the combatants in the fight that held up Game 3 of the 1973 NL Championship Series.

60. Name the only man to be in uniform for all 19 World Series games played by the Mets (through 1987).

61. In what World Series did the home team win every game?

62. How many world champions repeated during the 10-year span, 1978–87?

63. What is the record for most homers in a Championship Series, and which three players tie for the record?

64. Name the only man to get five hits in a World Series game.

65. What world champion had the worst winning percentage during the regular season?

66. What team won both the Championship Series and the World Series after trailing both by three games to one?

67. Identify the players from losing teams who won consecutive Most Valuable Player honors in the NL Championship Series.

68. When were the first indoor World Series games played?

69. Name the only teams that have never won a divisional championship.

70. Name the three Dodgers chosen co-MVPs of the 1981 World Series.

71. Name at least two seasons when the World Series was played on one field.

72. Who holds the record for consecutive scoreless innings pitched in a World Series?

73. Whose drive did Willie Mays catch with his back to the plate in the 1954 World Series?

This over-the-shoulder catch by Willie Mays during the 1954 World Series helped the Giants upset the favored Indians in four straight games.

74. Who was the only man to hit five homers in the same World Series?

75. How did a playoff help Eddie Mathews win a home-run crown?

• ANSWERS •

1. None.

2. Larry Sherry.

3. Darold Knowles of the Oakland Athletics, against the Mets in 1973.

4. He was caught stealing with two outs in the ninth inning and Bob Meusel at bat in a 3–2 game.

5.   Babe Ruth (twice) and Reggie Jackson.

6.   Willie Mays.

7.   Chuck Essegian.

8.   Bernie Carbo of the 1975 Red Sox.

9.   Casey Stengel of the Giants hit two during the 1923 Series.

10. Bill Mazeroski of the Pirates, in the home half of the ninth inning of Game 7 in 1960.

11. George Brett of the Royals, in Game 3 of the 1978 ALCS against the Yankees.

12. Mike Cuellar of the Orioles, on October 3, 1970, at Minnesota.

Left-handed screwball specialist Mike Cuellar was not known for his hitting ability.

13. The 1976 AL Championship Series between the Yankees and Royals ended when New York's Chris Chambliss led off the home ninth with a home run off Mark Littell.

14. Bob Gibson of the Cardinals, in the 1968 opener against Detroit.

15. Sal Maglie of the Dodgers.

16. Bucky Dent in 1978; ironically, Dent had hit only four homers that season.

17. Dusty Rhodes, who had hit .333 for the Giants as a pinch hitter during the 1954 regular season, hit

a three-run, 10th-inning pinch homer off Bob Lemon to win Game 1; a game-trying pinch single—followed by a later home run—in the fifth inning of Game 2; and a two-run pinch single in Game 3. Officially, he was 4 for 6 with 7 runs batted in.

18. Joe Coleman of the 1972 Tigers, and Mike Boddicker of the 1983 Orioles.

19. The 1982 Brewers and the 1984 Padres.

20. Carlton Fisk of the Red Sox.

21. The Philadelphia Athletics, down 8–0, scored 10 runs in the seventh inning of Game 4 against the Cubs, on October 12, 1929. The 10–8 victory gave them the momentum they needed to win the Series, four games to one, two days later.

22. Enos Slaughter of the 1946 Cardinals, against the Red Sox. A slight hesitation by shortstop Johnny Pesky in making the relay gave Slaughter the leeway he needed. Slaughter's dash in the home eighth of Game 7 gave St. Louis a 4–3 victory.

23. Dave McNally of the Orioles connected in the sixth inning of Game 3 against Cincinnati in 1970.

24. The 1924 Senators, 1958 Yankees, 1968 Tigers, 1979 Pirates, and 1985 Royals.

25. 1980, Phillies vs. Royals.

26. Cookie Lavagetto and Al Gionfriddo of the Dodgers and Floyd Bevens of the Yankees.

27. Charlie Root of the Cubs was Ruth's victim in the fifth inning of Game 3 in the 1932 World Series. Ruth, who had hit a three-run homer off Root in the first inning, took a strike, two balls, then another called strike. Then he apparently pointed—either toward center field or toward

the pitcher's mound—and followed with a long home run in the same general direction. The home run put the Yankees ahead, 5-4, in a game they eventually won, 7-5. New York swept the World Series.

28. Ernie Lombardi of the Reds failed to hold a throw from rightfielder Ival Goodman in Game 4 of the 1939 World Series against the Yankees. Just as Lombardi was trying to catch the ball, Charlie Keller crashed into him. As the stunned Lombardi fell backward, the ball rolled away, enabling Joe DiMaggio—who had hit the ball to Goodman—to circle the bases. The Yankees won the game, 7-4, to sweep the Series.

29. Mickey Owen of the Dodgers missed the third strike against the Yankees' Tommy Henrich with two outs and nobody on base and the Dodgers leading, 4-3, in Game 4 of the 1941 World Series. The Yankees then exploded for four runs to win, 7-4, and wrapped up the Series the next day.

30. Fred Snodgrass of the New York Giants dropped an easy fly ball from Boston's Clyde Engle, who led off the 10th inning of the eighth and final game of the 1912 World Series. Harry Hooper lined out to Snodgrass, but the next batter walked, putting two men on base. Tris Speaker's pop foul fell untouched before Speaker, given another chance, singled home the tying run. Larry Gardner's sacrifice fly then scored Steve Yerkes, who had walked, with the winning run of a 3-2 game. The Snodgrass error was called the "$30,000 Muff" because it denied his 16 teammates the difference between the winners' share of $4,025 and the losers' share of $2,566.

31. Ralph Terry of the Yankees threw a 1-0 pitch that Mazeroski hit out of Forbes Field in Pittsburgh, on October 13, 1960.

32.   Ken Boyer (Cards) and Clete Boyer (Yanks) in Game 7 in 1964.

33.   Christy Mathewson of the New York Giants blanked the Philadelphia Athletics, 3-0, 9-0, and 2-0 during the 1905 World Series.

34.   Red Sox pitcher Babe Ruth batted sixth in Game 4 of the 1918 World Series. In his last appearance as a World Series pitcher, Ruth hit a two-run triple to help beat the Cubs, 3-2. He finished the game in left field as Joe Bush nailed down the win.

35.   None.

36.   Chuck Hiller of the 1962 Giants hit one in the seventh inning of Game 4 against the Yankees. San Francisco won, 7-3.

37.   Duke Snider (Dodgers) and Willie Mays (Giants).

38.   Pee Wee Reese.

39.   Yogi Berra of the Yankees, in Game 3 of the 1947 World Series against the Dodgers, The victim was Ralph Branca.

40.   Dan Driessen of the Reds, in 1976, the first year the DH was used in the World Series. He batted .357 as Cincinnati swept the Yankees.

41.   Elmer Smith of the 1920 Indians, against the Dodgers.

42.   Mickey Mantle, 18.

Just as he did during the regular season, Mickey Mantle always swung a potent bat in October.

43.   Duke Snider, 11.

44.   Mickey Lolich, notoriously weak-hitting Detroit pitcher, homered in the third inning of World Series Game 2 against St. Louis in 1968. Nelson Briles was the victim. Lolich hit an anemic .110 during a career that spanned 16 seasons.

Detroit left-hander Mickey Lolich overshadowed 31-game winner Denny McLain, his Tiger teammate, during the 1968 World Series.

45.   Willie Mays Aikens of the Royals against the Phillies in 1980.

46.   The "miracle" Boston Braves of 1914 swept the Philadelphia Athletics.

47.   Mike Andrews, second baseman for the 1973 Oakland Athletics, made two errors in the 12th inning of Game 2 against the Mets. Upset Oakland owner Charles O. Finley tried to "deactivate" Andrews but was ordered to reinstate him by Commissioner Bowie Kuhn. With the Andrews affair the latest in a long list of Finley "offenses," Oakland manager Dick Williams told his players before Game 3 he would not return for the 1974 season.

48.   Bob Robertson of the Pirates, in Game 2 of the 1971 NLCS against the Giants.

49.   Lou Boudreau of the Indians led a winning effort in 1948.

50. George Brett of the Royals had three solo home runs in Game 3 of the 1978 ALCS against the Yankees, but New York prevailed, 6–5.

George Brett of the Royals always excels in postseason play.

51. After stealing a rookie-record 110 bases, the St. Louis leftfielder became entangled in the automated tarpaulin before NLCS Game 4 in St. Louis. He suffered a bone chip and contusions—injuries that kept him sidelined for the remainder of his team's postseason play. Replacement Tito Landrum, a journeyman outfielder, hit .360 in the World Series, which the Cardinals lost.

Vince Coleman, sidelined with an injury, missed the 1985 World Series after his sensational rookie season helped the Cardinals win a pennant.

52. Red Sox first baseman Bill Buckner allowed Mookie Wilson's two-out grounder to go through his

legs as Ray Knight raced home with the run that enabled the Mets to win Game 6 and set the stage for a come-from-behind World Series victory. The Mets scored three in the 10th to win Game 6, 6–5, then took Game 7, 8–5.

53.   Dave Henderson's shot off California's Donnie Moore enabled Boston to take a 6–5 lead over California in a game they eventually won, 7–6 in 11 innings at Anaheim Stadium. Returning to Fenway, the Bosox took 10–4 and 8–1 wins to ice the 1986 American League pennant.

54.   Ozzie Smith of the Cardinals homered in the ninth inning of NLCS Game 5 against Los Angeles in 1985 to give St. Louis a 3–2 victory and a 3–2 lead in the series. In the next game, on October 16 in Los Angeles, Jack Clark's three-run homer in the ninth gave the Cards a 7–5 win and the pennant. Both ninth-inning homers were yielded by Tom Niedenfuer.

55.   Reggie Jackson has appeared in 77 postseason games: 45 Championship Series games, 27 World Series games, and five divisional playoff games. Yogi Berra has appeared in the most World Series games, 75.

In his first year with the Yankees, Reggie Jackson was a one-man show in the World Series against the Dodgers.

56.   Tito Landrum of the Orioles hit a one-out, 10th-inning homer off Britt Burns of the White Sox to break up a scoreless tie. Baltimore scored two more runs in the inning to win 3–0 and take the pennant, three games to one. Landrum had been acquired by Baltimore one day before the cutoff date for postseason eligibility after he'd spent most of the year in the minors.

Journeyman outfielder Tito Landrum played for the Cardinals and Dodgers but belonged to an American League team when he became an October hero.

57.   Bob Moose of the Pirates uncorked the ninth-inning wild pitch that gave the Reds a 4–3 win in Game 5 of the 1972 NLCS. Johnny Bench had led off the inning with a game-tying homer off Dave Giusti. After Tony Perez and Denis Menke singled, Moose replaced Giusti and retired Cesar Geronimo and Darrel Chaney. Hal McRae was at bat when Moose uncorked his wild pitch, scoring George Foster, who had run for Perez.

58.   Bobby Richardson of the Yankees had 12 RBI during the 1960 World Series against Pittsburgh. After collecting only 26 RBI for the entire regular season, the light-hitting second baseman got six RBI, including a grand slam off Clem Labine, in Game 3. His two triples helped him get three more RBI in Game 6. In his career, Richardson never got as many as 60 RBI in a season.

59. Bud Harrelson of the Mets and Pete Rose of the Reds.

60. Bud Harrelson.

61. Twins vs Cardinals, 1987.

62. None.

63. Jeffrey Leonard of the 1987 Giants, Steve Garvey of the 1978 Dodgers, and Bob Robertson of the 1971 Pirates all hit four homers in a championship series.

64. Paul Molitor of the 1982 Brewers, against the Cardinals.

Paul Molitor was a hitting star for the losing Brewers in the 1982 World Series against St. Louis.

65. The 1987 Twins, 85–77, .525.

66. The 1985 Royals.

67. Mike Scott of the Astros and Jeffrey Leonard of the Giants won consecutive NLCS honors in 1986–87 respectively.

68. In 1987, when four games were played at the Hubert H. Humphrey Metrodome, home of the Twins.

69. The Texas Rangers, Seattle Mariners, and Cleveland Indians. All NL teams have won divisional titles.

70. Ron Cey, Steve Yeager, and Pedro Guerrero. Yeager and Guerrero both homered twice, Guerrero led the Dodgers with seven RBI, and Cey survived a Goose Gossage beaning to hit .350 for the Series, with two hits in the decisive sixth game.

71. In 1921–22, the last two seasons before Yankee Stadium opened, the Yankees were tenants of the Giants at the Polo Grounds. When both clubs won back-to-back pennants, the World Series had a permanent two-year home. In 1944, both St. Louis teams finished first, making Sportsman's Park the sole Series field.

72. Whitey Ford of the Yankees, 33-2/3.

Whitey Ford did his best pitching during the World Series.

73. Vic Wertz of the Indians hit the 460-foot smash with two men on in the eighth inning of Game 1 with the score tied at 2–2. The Giants eventually won the game, 5–2.

74. Reggie Jackson of the Yankees in 1977.

75. Before the advent of divisional play in 1969, end-of-season ties between teams were settled through pennant playoffs—a best-of-three se-

ries in the National League and a sudden-death single game in the American. Statistics from those games counted as part of the regular-season stats, although Championship Series statistics are kept separately. In 1959, when the Milwaukee Braves lost a two-game playoff to the Los Angeles Dodgers, Eddie Mathews of the Braves homered to break a deadlock for the home-run crown with Ernie Banks of the Cubs. Mathews thus won that year's home run crown, 46 to 45.

• 8 •

ALL-STAR TRIVIA

When the All-Star Game was initially suggested as a one-time-only "dream game" between the stars of the two major leagues, baseball club owners turned a cold shoulder toward the concept. They reasoned that a three-day midseason break for what they deemed merely an exhibition game would hurt attendance.

Only through the persistence of Commissioner Kenesaw Mountain Landis and the league presidents, John Heydler (National) and Will Harridge (American), was the game approved.

No thought was given to an annual All-Star Game until overwhelming fan reaction compelled a renewal of the matchup.

An informal fan poll provided "guidelines" for the managers, who were still free to select their own 18-man squads for that first game in 1933. Fourteen of the 36 men selected eventually wound up in the Baseball Hall of Fame.

Controversy has followed the All-Star selection process almost from its inception. The method of selection has been changed several times—once by the commissioner after two straight years of obvious ballot-box stuffing by Cincinnati partisans.

From 1958 to 1969, players, coaches, and managers picked the starters under a system that ensured fairness; they were barred from voting for teammates. In 1970, however, Commissioner Bowie Kuhn restored the fan vote. A chorus of critics has since charged that the All-Star election is merely a popularity contest that often ignores deserving players.

There have been many highlights in All-Star play: the dramatic home runs of Ted Williams, the baserunning of Pete Rose, the dramatic flair of Willie Mays, and the pitching of Carl Hubbell. All-Star play is baseball at its best.

• SCORING •

Are you an All-Star in baseball trivia? Grade your expertise:

28–30	Grade A. Excellent knowledge of both leagues.
24–27	Grade B. Good enough to coach, but not manage.
21–23	Grade C. Capable of picking a good backup squad.
18–20	Grade D. Hardly All-Star caliber.
Under 18	Grade F. Anemic statistics don't lie.

• QUESTIONS •

1. Who started All-Star Games at five different positions?

2. Who had two wins and two saves over a four-game All-Star streak?

3. Whose .169 batting average was the lowest ever for an All-Star starter?

4. Whose home run won the first All-Star Game?

5. Why was the 1945 All-Star Game canceled?

6. Why were two All-Star Games played for several years?

7. How are All-Star managers chosen?

8. What All-Star Game drew 72,000 fans?

9. What brothers homered in All-Star Games?

10. Name the only pitcher to start two All-Star Games in one year.

11. Who yielded Ted Williams's ninth-inning All-Star homer?

12. Who was blown off the mound during an All-Star Game?

13. Who won an All-Star Game without throwing a pitch?

14. Name the first player to homer twice in one All-Star Game.

15. Who hit the only grand slam in All-Star Game history?

16. Name the only brother battery to start an All-Star Game.

17. Name the first rookie to play in an All-Star Game.

18. Name the only write-ins elected to the starting lineup since the fan vote was restored in 1970.

19. Name the only pitcher to win three All-Star Games.

20. Who was the only player to be an All-Star for four different teams?

21. Who was the only player to appear twice in the same Midsummer Classic?

22. Who played in the most All-Star Games?

Hank Aaron's second All-Star homer was hit in his home park, Atlanta–Fulton County Stadium.

23. Name one of the two pitchers to win an All-Star Game, World Series Game, and the Cy Young Award in the same season.

AMERICAN LEAGUE ALL-STAR TEAM
1933

(Top Row) SHARKEY, CONROY, GEHRIG, RUTH, HILDEBRAND, MACK, CRONIN, GROVE, SHARKEY, DICKEY, SIMMONS, GOMEZ. WES.FERRELL, DYKES, SHARKEY.

(Bottom Row) SCHACHT, COLLINS, LAZZERI, CROWDER, FOXX, FLETCHER, AVERILL, ROMMEL, CHAPMAN, FERRELL. WEST, GEHRINGER. McBRIDE.

NATIONAL LEAGUE ALL-STAR TEAM
1933

(Top Row) HARTNETT, WILSON, FRISH, HUBBELL, WALKER, WANER, ENGLISH, SCHUMACHER, TRAYNOR, LOTSHAW.

(Middle Row) HALLAHAN, BARTELL, TERRY, McKECHNIE, McGRAW, CAREY, HAFEY, KLEIN, O'DOUL, BERGER.

(Bottom Row) HASBROOK, MARTIN, WARNEKE, CUCCINELLO .

24. Who was the only non-Red elected when Cincinnati fans stuffed the All-Star ballot boxes in 1957?

25. Whose idea launched the All-Star Game?

26. Name two pitchers who struck out five straight hitters in the All-Star Game.

27. Name the first father and son to be All-Stars.

28. What player who went homerless during the regular season hit a pinch homer in the All-Star Game?

29. What catcher was the victim of the Pete Rose body block that won the 1970 All-Star Game?

30. Name the only NL manager to lose three All-Star Games.

• ANSWERS •

1. Pete Rose started at first base, second base, third base, left field, and right field.

2. Bruce Sutter, 1978–81.

3. Davey Lopes of the Dodgers started the August 9 All-Star Game in the strike year of 1981. His average was .169 when the seven-week strike began, but he won the All-Star berth in the fan vote because of excellent name recognition.

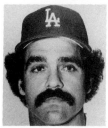

Though he was a fine all-around player, Davey Lopes held a dubious distinction in All-Star annals.

4. Babe Ruth of the Yankees hit a two-run homer in the sixth inning of the 1933 All-Star Game to give the AL a 4–2 victory.

Babe Ruth's two-run homer helped the American League win the first All-Star Game. Lou Gehrig (left) and batboy John McBride greeted Ruth as he touched the plate.

5. Wartime travel restrictions scrubbed the game. Many teams played exhibitions instead.

6. To raise money for the players' pension fund, two All-Star Games were played from 1959 to 1962.

7. They are the managers whose teams won pennants the previous year.

8. The 1981 All-Star Game in Cleveland drew the record crowd because it marked the return of baseball after the game's most devastating strike.

9. The DiMaggios. Joe of the Yankees helped the AL to a 3–1 win in 1939, and Vince of the Pirates homered in a 5–3 NL defeat in 1943.

10. Don Drysdale of the Dodgers, in 1959.

11. Claude Passeau of the Cubs gave up the two-out, three-run blast at Detroit's Briggs Stadium, allowing the AL to pull out a 7–5 win in the 1941 All-Star Game.

12. Stu Miller of the Giants, during the July 11, 1961, game in Candlestick Park, committed an unintentional balk, moving inherited baserunners up to second and third, when the wind blew him off the mound. A Ken Boyer error allowed the AL to score its second run of the ninth inning to tie the game, 3–3. The AL scored again in the 10th, but the Nationals scored twice in the home 10th to win, 5–4. Miller was the winning pitcher.

13. Dean Stone of the Senators entered the 1954 All-Star Game at Cleveland with two outs in the top of the eighth and the AL behind, 9–8. Red Schoendienst tried to steal home with Duke Snider at bat, but Stone was able to throw to catcher Yogi Berra in time to nail Schoendienst for the third out. In the home eighth, Stone was lifted for pinch hitter Larry Doby, who homered to tie the game. Two more runs scored on a Texas Leaguer by Nellie Fox, and the AL had an 11–9 victory. Stone was the pitcher of record even though he had not thrown a pitch.

14. Arky Vaughan, Pittsburgh shortstop, hit two homers for the NL in 1941.

15. Fred Lynn of the Angels, in 1983's 50th anniversary All-Star Game at Chicago's Comiskey Park, in the third inning of a 13–3 victory. The victim was Atlee Hammaker of the Giants, who yielded seven earned runs in two-thirds of an inning pitched.

16. Mort and Walker Cooper of the Cardinals started for the NL in 1942–43.

17. Joe DiMaggio of the Yankees in 1936. He went 0 for 5 and made an error.

18. Rico Carty of the Braves in 1970 and Steve Garvey of the Dodgers in 1974.

19. Lefty Gomez of the Yankees, in 1933–35–37.

20. Goose Gossage, with the White Sox, Pirates, Yankees, and Padres.

21. In 1934, Cub second baseman Billy Herman popped out in the third inning as a pinch hitter for Carl Hubbell, then reappeared in the seventh when AL manager Joe Cronin OK'd NL manager Bill Terry's request to allow Herman to replace charley-horse victim Frankie Frisch.

22. Hank Aaron, Stan Musial, and Willie Mays each appeared in 24 games.

23. Vern Law of the 1960 Pirates and Sandy Koufax of the 1965 Dodgers completed this rare "triple."

24. St. Louis first baseman Stan Musial. Commissioner Ford Frick, annoyed by the ballot stuffing, replaced elected Cincinnati starters Gus Bell and Wally Post with Willie Mays (Giants) and Hank Aaron (Braves), respectively. He also returned the vote to players, coaches, and managers in 1958.

25. Arch Ward, *Chicago Tribune* sports editor, conceived the "dream game" idea as a one-time-only event to coincide with Chicago's Century of Progress exposition, the 1933 world's fair.

26. Carl Hubbell of the Giants in 1934 and Fernando Valenzuela of the Dodgers in 1986. Hubbell fanned future Hall of Famers Babe Ruth, Lou Gehrig, Jimmie Foxx, Al Simmons, and Joe Cronin; Valenzuela whiffed Don Mattingly, Cal Ripken Jr., Jesse Barfield, Lou Whitaker, and Teddy Higuera.

27. Gus and Buddy Bell. Gus played in four games during the 1950s, and Buddy became a first-time All-Star in 1983.

28. Mickey Owen of the Dodgers, in 1942. He went homerless in 133 regular-season games.

29.   Ray Fosse of the Indians.

30.   Whitey Herzog of the Cardinals.

Carl Hubbell (right), with fellow New York Giants pitchers Bill Lohr-man, Harry Gumbert, and Cliff Melton (left to right), threw so many screwballs during an illustrious career that his left wrist and hand were permanently turned inward.

· 9 ·
AWARDS

Baseball honors its best players with a series of awards at the end of each season. Members of the media vote for the Most Valuable Player in each league, as well as for the Rookie of the Year, Cy Young Award winner, Manager of the Year, and Comeback Player of the Year.

Several publications, including *The Sporting News*, present their own awards, including postseason All-Star selections that provide a better perspective on player performance than the midseason fan choices who play in the All-Star Game.

Award winners often come from contending clubs, but there have been exceptions in every major award category. League statistical leaders in batting and pitching command considerable attention when electors vote for awards, but even individual champions sometimes fall short.

Maury Wills was named National League MVP when he broke Ty Cobb's single-season record with 104 stolen bases in 1962, but Lou Brock failed to win the award when he stole 118 times in 1974. Both played for clubs that narrowly missed finishing first.

Willie Stargell was deprived in 1973, when he had 44 homers, 119 runs batted in, and a .646 slugging average for the near-miss Pirates. MVP honors went to batting champion Pete Rose, who had a .338 average, five homers, and 64 RBI. Reason: Cincinnati won its division.

Even Triple Crown winners don't necessarily win MVP Awards; on three different occasions, Triple Crown winners have been also-rans in MVP voting.

The first MVPs were World Series opponents Lefty Grove (Athletics) and Frankie Frisch (Cardinals) in 1931. Their selection established a precedent of giving awards to players from championship clubs.

• SCORING •

Earn an award for your knowledge of baseball awards. Use this guide:

36–40   Grade A. Congratulations, you're the first Triple Crown winner since Carl Yastrzemski.

31–35   Grade B. Future MVP potential.

26–30   Grade C. Rookie of the Year.

21–25   Grade D. Candidate for Comeback of the Year—try the next chapter.

Under 21   Grade F. Stay tuned for the booby prize.

• QUESTIONS •

1.   Name the only player to be Most Valuable Player in both leagues.

2.   Name the only pitcher to win the Cy Young Award in both leagues.

3.   Name the only pitcher to win the Cy Young Award four times.

4.   Name the first winner of the Cy Young Award.

5.   Name the first winner of the Rookie of the Year Award.

6.   Name the only pitcher to win the Cy Young and Rookie of the Year Awards in the same season.

7.   Name the only player to win the MVP and Rookie of the Year Awards in the same season.

8.   Name the only Giant to win the Cy Young Award.

9.   Name two active players who have won consecutive MVP Awards.

10.   Who was the first relief pitcher to win the Cy Young Award?

11.   Name the only relievers to sweep the Cy Young and MVP Awards.

12.   Name a four-time winner of the Most Valuable Player Award.

13.   Who was the last switch hitter to be American League MVP?

14. This three-time MVP was shelved by an off-season automobile wreck.

15. What two-time MVP holds the record for home runs by a shortstop?

16. What are the qualifications for being on the Rookie of the Year Award ballot?

17. Name the only pitcher to win consecutive MVP awards.

18. What two-time AL home-run king was replaced by Lou Gehrig?

19. Name the only brothers to win the Cy Young Award.

20. Who was American League MVP the year before Roger Maris hit 61 homers?

21. Name the two players who won MVP Awards at different positions.

22. Name the only pitcher to win the Cy Young Award while pitching for a last-place team.

23. Name the only pitcher to win the Cy Young Award in his last season.

24. Name the two MVPs whose teams lost more than they won.

25. Who was the only reliever to win an MVP Award without winning a Cy Young Award.

26. How many Cy Young Awards has Nolan Ryan won?

27. Name the only MVP from a last-place club.

28. Name the only members of the 30/30 Club (30 steals, 30 homers) who also won MVP Awards.

29. Who was the only player to win simultaneous MVP honors for the season, the Championship Series, and the World Series?

30. When was the MVP Award started?

31. What are the qualifications for the batting crown?

32. Who was the first unanimous choice for the Cy Young Award?

33. Who was the first unanimous choice for the Rookie of the Year Award?

34. Who was the first unanimous choice for the Most Valuable Player Award?

35. Name two players who won the Triple Crown but lost the MVP that year.

36. Why were three Cy Young Awards given in one year?

37. Only once have pitchers swept Cy Young and MVP honors in both leagues during the same season. Name the players involved.

38.   Who interrupted Dale Murphy's bid to become the first player to win three straight MVP Awards?

39.   How many times was Hank Aaron voted Most Valuable Player?

40.   A nine-vote margin kept this star from becoming the only player to win a fourth MVP Award. Who was he?

• ANSWERS •

1.   Frank Robinson of the 1961 Reds and 1966 Orioles.

2.   Gaylord Perry of the 1972 Indians and 1978 Padres.

Right-hander Gaylord Perry won more than 300 games while pitching for numerous clubs.

3.   Steve Carlton of the Phillies.

4.   Don Newcombe of the Dodgers, in 1956. Only one major-league pitcher received the Cy

Young Award from its inception until 1967, when awards were presented to one pitcher in each league.

5. Jackie Robinson of the Dodgers in 1947. Single rookie awards were bestowed until 1949, when one player from each league was cited.

6. Fernando Valenzuela of the Dodgers.

Fernando Valenzuela refused to let a seven-week strike mar his rookie season.

7. Fred Lynn of the 1974 Red Sox.

While with the Red Sox, Fred Lynn staged a two-man race for the Rookie of the Year Award with teammate and fellow outfielder Jim Rice.

8. Mike McCormick, 1967.

9. Dale Murphy of the 1982–83 Braves, and Mike Schmidt of the 1980–81 Phillies.

10. Mike Marshall of the 1974 Dodgers.

11. Willie Hernandez of the 1984 Tigers and Rollie Fingers of the 1981 Brewers.

12. No one has ever won four MVP Awards.

13. Vida Blue, Oakland pitcher, in 1971.

Vida Blue is the only pitcher to start an All-Star Game for each league.

14. Roy Campanella of the Dodgers, who last played in 1957.

15. Ernie Banks of the Cubs hit 47 home runs, a shortstop record, in 1958.

16. To qualify for rookie status a player must not have exceeded 130 at-bats or 50 innings pitched in the majors during a previous season or seasons, nor spent more than 45 days on a major-league roster during the 25-player limit (rosters expand to 40 players on September 1).

17. Hal Newhouser of the Tigers, 1944–45.

18. Wally Pipp, who yielded to Gehrig on June 2, 1925. Gehrig had pinch hit the previous day, so June 2 became Game 2 in his streak of 2,130 consecutive games played.

19. Jim and Gaylord Perry. Jim won with the 1970 Twins, Gaylord with the 1972 Indians and 1978 Padres.

20. Roger Maris.

21. Hank Greenberg won as first baseman for the 1935 Tigers and as an outfielder for the same team five years later; Stan Musial won as an outfielder for the 1943 Cardinals and as a first baseman for the 1946 team.

22. Steve Carlton of the 1972 Phillies. He won 27 of the team's 59 victories.

23. Sandy Koufax of the 1966 Dodgers. Though he was 27-9, with 317 strikeouts and a 1.73 ERA, he retired at age 30 with an arthritic elbow.

24. Ernie Banks of the 1958-59 Cubs, and Andre Dawson of the 1987 Cubs.

25. Jim Konstanty of the 1950 Phillies. The Cy Young Award did not exist until six years later.

26. None.

27. Andre Dawson of the 1987 Cubs, last in the NL East.

Andre Dawson was named Most Valuable Player a year after deserting the Montreal Expos for the Chicago Cubs via free agency.

28. Hank Aaron, Willie Mays, and Dale Murphy.

29. Willie Stargell of the 1979 Pirates. He shared NL MVP honors with Keith Hernandez of the Cardinals, in the only tie vote in the history of the MVP voting.

30. The award now recognized as the official MVP was first given by the Baseball Writers Association of America (BBWAA) in 1931. League awards were given by the AL, 1922–29, and by the NL, 1924–29. The Chalmers Automobile Company honored one player from each league for four years, 1911–14.

31. The batting champion is the player with the highest batting average based on a minimum of 502 appearances at the plate. Those appearances may include walks, sacrifices, hit by pitcher, etc.

32. Sandy Koufax of the 1963 Dodgers.

33. Frank Robinson of the 1956 Reds.

34. Hank Greenberg of the 1935 Tigers.

35. Ted Williams (twice) and Lou Gehrig. Williams won the Triple Crown in 1942 and 1947 but lost the MVP Award to Joe Gordon and Joe DiMaggio, respectively. Williams was named MVP in 1946 and 1949. In 1934 Gehrig's Triple Crown was not enough to keep Mickey Cochrane from winning the MVP Award.

36. In 1969, when Tom Seaver of the Mets won the first of his three NL Cy Young Awards, the American League had two winners: repeater Denny McLain of the Tigers tied Baltimore's Mike Cuellar in the voting. It was the only tie ever produced in the Cy Young Award voting.

37.   Bob Gibson of the Cardinals and Denny McLain of the Tigers, in 1968.

38.   Ryne Sandberg of the Cubs, 1984.

Ryne Sandberg became an all-around star for the Cubs after he was acquired from the Phillies.

39.   Once, in 1957.

40.   Three-time winner Stan Musial finished nine votes behind Hank Aaron in 1957.

· 10 ·
COOPERSTOWN

Not many years ago, young baseball writer Mike Schuman of Keene, New Hampshire, wrote in awe of his first visit to the Baseball Hall of Fame:

"Walking into the actual Hall of Fame is not unlike entering the Rotunda of the Capitol or Independence Hall. The designers of the Hall didn't monkey around when building this shrine to the immortals.

"Solemnity overtakes the atmosphere as one enters the wing, with its 25-foot-high ceiling and its marble columns. The plaques belonging to each of baseball's greats line the walls to the right and left. On each plaque are the player's greatest accomplishments in nutshell form.

"Whether it's the facts and figures on the walls, or seeing the names and faces of the best of the best, or simply the monumental architecture of the place, one can't leave the Hall without being just somewhat inspired."

Willie Stargell became Cooperstown's 200th inductee when he was enshrined on July 31, 1988. To win election, candidates must receive 75 percent of the vote cast by Hall of Fame electors.

Getting past those electors is not easy. Even Ty Cobb received "only" 98.2 percent of the vote (he was absent from four of the 226 ballots cast in 1936).

The four-story brick museum and adjacent baseball library at Cooperstown honor not only the relative handful of Hall of Famers but the game itself. Exhibits trace the game's history from pre–Civil War sandlot days through the development of domed ballparks.

The exploits of the Cooperstown 200 are so mind-boggling that they often seem larger than life. If you know baseball, answering the questions that follow won't be as tough as hitting a curveball.

In the Cooperstown Room of the Baseball Hall of Fame and Museum, displays combine photographs, original paintings, and an audio-visual presentation to depict the origin of the game. Previous year induction ceremonies are featured, with emphasis on the original 1939 dedication.

• SCORING •

Are you a candidate for the Cooperstown of trivia? Judge for yourself:

65–75   Grade A. You've earned a niche in the gallery.

60–64   Grade B. Keep plugging; you have Hall of Fame potential.

55–59   Grade C. You'll need a ticket to get into Cooperstown.

50–54   Grade D. You need a refresher course in baseball history.

Under 50   Grade F. You've made the Hall of Shame!

• QUESTIONS •

1. Why did the press ignore Lou Gehrig's four-homer game of 1932?

2. Name the only relief pitcher in the Hall of Fame.

3. Who hit the "Homer in the gloamin'"?

4. Who stole six bases in a game twice in a season?

5. Why is the Hall of Fame in Cooperstown?

6. Name the first five players enshrined.

7. A serious beaning ended this Hall of Famer's playing career.

8.   Whose childhood farm mishap enabled him to develop a Hall of Fame curveball?

9.   Who was the "Meal Ticket"?

10. Who blocked Jimmie Foxx's bid for a second straight Triple Crown?

11. Name a Hall of Famer who spent 25 years in the majors.

12. What Hall of Fame slugger lifted his right foot to get more muscle behind the ball?

13. What Hall of Famer led all pitchers in yielding Hank Aaron home runs?

14. Name the only Cooperstown inductee of 1988.

15. What Hall of Famer had the most home runs without ever leading his league?

16. Name the only player to hit .400 and 40 homers in the same season.

17. Name the only player to average .400 over a five-year span.

18. What two Hall of Famers shared home-run titles with each other twice?

19. This Hall of Famer had the only 50-homer season that also featured fewer than 50 strikeouts.

20. What Hall of Fame catcher made a sensational debut as a pitcher?

21. When Bob Feller no-hit the Yankees in 1946, what future Hall of Fame pitcher played center field?

22. Name the only man in both the baseball and football Halls of Fame.

In the Ballparks Room at the Baseball Hall of Fame and Museum, Ebbets Field, the Polo Grounds, Forbes Field, Shibe Park, and Crosley Field all come alive once again. These relics of the past, complete with original turnstiles, lockers, dugout benches, and grandstand seats, were the forerunners of today's multipurpose, computerized stadia, which are also represented there.

23. How did Tris Speaker revolutionize outfield play?

24. Name the only Hall of Famer whose career run total was greater than his total number of games.

25. What Hall of Famer holds the lifetime major-league record for triples?

26. Who stole the most bases in his career?

27. Who stole home the most times?

28. Who holds the major-league career RBI record?

29. .Who had the most .300 seasons?

30. What Hall of Famer was known for his foot-in-the-bucket stance?

31. Name the only three-time MVP not in the Hall of Fame.

32. Name two 500-homer hitters not in the Hall of Fame.

33. Who pitched the most career shutouts?

34. Who had the most 20-win seasons?

35. Name two Hall of Famers who homered in their first at-bat.

36. How many openers did Sandy Koufax pitch?

37. Who hit the most homers during a batting-title season?

38. Who is the top left-handed home-run hitter in NL history?

39. Name the only 1934 All-Star starter not in Cooperstown.

40. Who was the youngest player to get 3,000 hits?

41. What switch hitter hit the most lifetime home runs?

42. Who played Babe Ruth in the Lou Gehrig Story, *Pride of the Yankees*?

43. How many Hall of Fame candidates have been enshrined on their first try?

44. What Hall of Famer holds the record for hits by a rookie?

45. Name the only player to lead both leagues in home runs.

46. Though he was known for wearing number 44, Hank Aaron wore another number as a 1954 rookie. What was it?

47. Did Babe Ruth ever bat right-handed?

Though he looked surprised that he missed this pitch, Babe Ruth was a frequent strikeout victim.

48. What pitcher won the most consecutive games in a season?

49. Name the only losing pitcher in Cooperstown.

50. Has the Hall of Fame ever had a unanimous selection?

51. Why was 56 a lucky number for Joe DiMaggio?

52. Why was Joe DiMaggio considered the best pure hitter?

53. Was Joe DiMaggio elected to Cooperstown on his first try?

54. What Hall of Famer devised the first score-keeping system?

55. How many last-day hits did Ted Williams get when he hit .406?

56. What Hall of Famer homered in his last at-bat?

57. Who got the most total bases in a season?

58. In his National League debut, this future Hall of Famer gave up a home run to Babe Ruth. Name him.

59. What Hall of Famer yielded Willie Mays's first home run?

60. Did Babe Ruth ever lead his league in earned-run average?

61. Name the only player to win more than two titles in each component of the Triple Crown.

62. What Hall of Fame pitcher once got a $5,000 bonus for his hitting?

63. Though known as a second baseman, Jackie Robinson broke into the majors at what position?

64. Why did Mickey Mantle become a switch hitter?

65. Which Hall of Famer's debut did Clay Dalrymple spoil by getting the only hit?

66. What Hall of Famer was scouted by a U.S. senator?

67. What third-string catcher gave invaluable advice to Sandy Koufax?

68. Name one of the two pitchers with career ERAs under 2.00.

69. Who compiled the best earned-run average in a season?

70. This Hall of Famer was the only man to play, coach, and manage for the Atlanta Braves.

71. Name the former White Sox infielder who missed enshrinement in the Hall of Fame by a fraction of a percentage point.

72. What Hall of Fame shortstop liked to hit deliberate foul balls on pitches he didn't like?

73.   What teenager came off an Iowa farm to be-
       come an immediate star pitcher?

74.   What position has the most representatives in
       Cooperstown?

75.   What position has the fewest representatives in
       Cooperstown?

• ANSWERS •

1.   On June 3, 1932, the day Lou Gehrig hit four
      home runs in a game, John McGraw an-
      nounced his retirement as manager of the New
      York Giants, the team he had guided since 1902.

2.   Hoyt Wilhelm.

3.   On September 27, 1938, the Cubs were a game-
      and-a-half behind the Pirates as the two clubs
      began a crucial three-game series at Chicago's
      Wrigley Field. Dizzy Dean won a 2–1 opener for
      Chicago to narrow the gap to a half-game. In
      the second meeting the score was 5–5 with two
      outs in the ninth when Gabby Hartnett came to
      bat. Darkness and haze threatened to suspend
      play, but the 37-year-old playing manager
      slammed a homer—barely visible in the fading
      light—to win the game and catapult the Cubs
      into first place. The Cubs took the third game,
      10–1, and went on to the National League title.
      Hartnett's "homer in the gloamin' " was the turn-
      ing point.

4.   Eddie Collins of the Philadelphia Athletics, on
      September 11 and 22, 1912.

5.   The sleepy upstate New York village of Coopers-
      town—halfway between Utica and Schenec-
      tady—was chosen as the site for the Hall of

In the General History section of the Baseball Hall of Fame and Museum, more than 1,000 personal artifacts, photographs, and memorabilia present the history of the game: the Gas House Gang is there, along with the Bronx Bombers, the Miracle Mets and the Miracle Braves, the Hitless Wonders, and the Brooklyn Bums. Big Poison, Double XX, the Yankee Clipper, Dizzy, Cap, The Big Train, Yogi, Pie, Stan the Man, Cool Papa, Connie Mack, Ty Cobb, and Cy Young are prominently featured.

Fame and Museum because a special commission reported in 1907 that Abner Doubleday had "invented" baseball there. But Doubleday, a West Point plebe at the time, did not even visit Cooperstown in 1839. Because of the legend, however, the Hall of Fame opened in Cooperstown in 1939, 100 years after the alleged "invention."

6. Ty Cobb, Babe Ruth, Christy Mathewson, Walter Johnson, and Honus Wagner.

7. Mickey Cochrane of the Tigers, in 1937.

8. Mordecai (Three-Finger) Brown of the Cubs had six straight 20-win seasons and pitched Chicago to pennants in 1906–07–08 and in 1910. He lost

parts of two fingers in a feed cutter but used the handicap to develop one of baseball's greatest curveballs.

9. Carl Hubbell, star left-hander of the New York Giants, led the team to three flags and two near misses during a five-year span in the 1930s. He was named MVP in two of those seasons.

Carl Hubbell won 253 games and two Most Valuable Player awards during his tenure with the New York Giants.

10. In 1938, when Foxx hit 50 homers for the second time, Hank Greenberg hit eight more to win the home-run title.

11. Eddie Collins.

12. Mel Ott of the New York Giants.

13. Don Drysdale of the Dodgers gave up 17 Aaron homers.

14. Willie Stargell.

15. Stan Musial of the Cardinals hit 475 homers but never more than 39 in a season.

16. Rogers Hornsby of the Cardinals hit .401 with 42 homers and 152 RBI in 1922.

17. Rogers Hornsby of the Cardinals averaged better than .400 from 1921 to 1925.

18. Johnny Mize of the Giants and Ralph Kiner of the Pirates shared NL home-run honors for two consecutive seasons, 1947–48, with totals of 51 and 40, respectively.

19. Johnny Mize of the Giants had 51 homers and 42 strikeouts in 1947.

20. Roger Bresnahan was with Washington of the National League when he blanked the Cardinals, 3–0, on August 27, 1897, in his big-league pitching debut.

21. Bob Lemon.

22. Umpire Cal Hubbard, once a standout football lineman.

23. Speaker, the longtime star of the Indians, played a shallow center field, which allowed him to get more assists—449—than any other outfielder. He twice had an AL record 35 assists. Speaker could also hit; his lifetime batting average was .344. The major-league record for single-season assists is held by the Phillies' Chuck Klein, with 44.

24. Outfielder Billy Hamilton scored 1,690 runs in 1,578 games, 1888–1901. He had 12 straight .300 seasons and a .344 career average.

25. Wahoo Sam Crawford, a .309 lifetime hitter, had 312 lifetime triples, mostly for the Detroit Tigers. He led the league in that department six times before retiring in 1917.

26. Lou Brock swiped 938, most of them for the Cardinals.

27. Ty Cobb, 50 times.

28. Hank Aaron knocked in 2,297 runs.

29. Ty Cobb, 23.

30. Al Simmons of the Philadelphia Athletics. He was a great clutch hitter who produced 11 straight .300 seasons despite his unorthodox batting stance. He had more hits than any right-handed batter in AL history except Al Kaline. Simmons, whose rookie season was 1924, won two batting crowns.

31. Mike Schmidt.

32. Mike Schmidt and Reggie Jackson.

The Great Moments Room of the Baseball Hall of Fame and Museum features Ruth's 60th homer, Maris's 61st, Aaron's 715th, and one by Thomson; Williams batting .406, DiMaggio hitting safely in 56, and Gehrig playing in 2,130; Robinson's debut and Brock's finale; no-hitters by Koufax, Haddix, Vander Meer, and Feller; and Drysdale shutting out the opposition for 58-2/3 consecutive innings.

33. Walter Johnson of the Senators, 110.

34. Cy Young had 16, Warren Spahn and Christy Mathewson 13 each.

35.   Earl Averill of the Indians, on April 16, 1929; and
       Hoyt Wilhelm of the Giants, on April 23, 1952.

36.   One, on April 14, 1964. He beat St. Louis, 4–0, at
       Los Angeles.

37.   Mickey Mantle of the Yankees hit 52 home runs
       while batting .353 during his Triple Crown season
       of 1956.

38.   Willie McCovey, 521.

39.   Wally Berger of the Boston Braves, who batted
       fifth and played center field for the NL.

40.   Ty Cobb was 34 on August 18, 1921, when he got
       his 3,000th. The victim was Boston's Elmer Myers.

41.   Mickey Mantle, 536.

42.   Babe Ruth.

43.   In 1988 Willie Stargell became the 17th.

44.   Lloyd Waner of the 1927 Pirates, 223.

45.   Wahoo Sam Crawford, one of the greatest
       sluggers of the dead-ball era, hit 16 for the 1902
       Reds to lead the NL and seven for the 1908 Tigers
       to lead the AL.

46.   5.

47.   Yes. On May 21, 1930, in a game at Shibe Park
       against the Philadelphia Athletics, Ruth faced
       spitballer Jack Quinn in the ninth inning after
       hitting three previous home runs. Though Quinn
       was a right-hander who might have been easy
       prey for a left-handed slugger in search of a
       record-tying fourth home run, Ruth decided to
       bat right-handed against him. He took two
       called strikes before reverting to his natural left-
       handed stance. Quinn then proceeded to strike
       him out.

48. Rube Marquard won 19 straight for the 1912 New York Giants, then went 7–11 for the rest of the season.

49. Satchel Paige, 28–31 in the majors, was enshrined because of his many years of stardom in the Negro Leagues. Paige, a major-league rookie at age 42 in 1948, was rated by many who saw him in his prime as the greatest pitcher in baseball history.

50. No. All-time home-run king Hank Aaron received 97.8 percent of the vote, second highest percentage to Ty Cobb's, but was left off nine ballots. When Willie Mays was chosen, 23 writers omitted his name.

51. During Joe DiMaggio's record 56-game hitting streak between May 15 and July 16, 1941, the Yankee centerfielder also collected 56 singles and scored 56 runs—making the number 56 particularly lucky for him.

52. In a career that stretched 13 years from 1936 to 1951, Joe DiMaggio hit .325 with 361 home runs. He had seven 30-homer seasons and nine 100-RBI campaigns. He was regarded as a pure hitter because he almost always made contact. Of baseball's great sluggers, DiMaggio ranks first in home run–to–strikeout ratio with a .978 mark (369 lifetime strikeouts). Yogi Berra ranks second and Ted Williams third. DiMaggio was especially impressive as a contact hitter in 1941, when he fanned just 13 times while hitting 30 home runs in 541 at-bats.

53. No. Though he retired after the 1951 season and was eligible a year later under rules existing at that time. DiMaggio fell 71 votes short because the electors were busy catching up on the enshrinement of old-timers. Dizzy Dean and Al Sim-

In the Directory Room of the Baseball Hall of Fame and Museum, color photos of today's stars greet the visitor. A large directory board provides guidance to the contents of the museum's four floors.

mons were voted in during DiMaggio's first year of eligibility, then Rabbit Maranville, Bill Dickey, and Bill Terry made it the next year, with DiMaggio 14 votes short. He was elected on his third try.

54. English-born baseball writer Henry Chadwick devised the first system of scoring and created the forerunner of the box score. Chadwick, the longtime rules chairman of the National Baseball Association, began his baseball writing in 1858, two years before Abraham Lincoln got the news of his presidential nomination while playing in an amateur baseball game.

55. Six, in a season-ending doubleheader on September 28, 1941.

56. Ted Williams of the Red Sox, on September 26, 1960.

57. Babe Ruth of the Yankees, 457 in 1921.

58.　Carl Hubbell of the New York Giants.

59.　Warren Spahn of the Boston Braves.

60.　Yes. His 1.75 ERA for the 1916 Red Sox led the AL.

61.　Ted Williams of the Red Sox won six batting titles, six home-run crowns, and four RBI championships.

62.　Jim (Catfish) Hunter of the Athletics.

63.　First base.

64.　A natural right-hander, Mantle learned to switch hit at the suggestion of his father, Elven (Mutt) Mantle. The idea paid off: Mantle hit home runs both left- and right-handed in the same game a record 10 times. The first switch-hitter, Robert Ferguson of the New York Mutuals (later Giants), played in 1871. Among the great switch hitters who followed were Max Carey, Frankie Frisch, Red Schoendienst, Maury Wills, Pete Rose, Ted Simmons, Willie Wilson, and Eddie Murray.

65.　Juan Marichal of the Giants yielded a two-out pinch single in the eighth to Dalrymple on July 19, 1960. San Francisco won the one-hitter, 2–0.

66.　Harmon Killebrew. When Killebrew was growing up in Payette, Idaho, U.S. Senator Herman Welker saw him play. Welker, a close friend of Washington Senators owner Calvin Griffith, advised the baseball magnate of his talented find. Griffith followed up and signed the young slugger. In 1959, Killebrew's first full season, he hit a league-leading 42 home runs at age 23. He went on to hit .573, fifth on the career list.

67.　Norm Sherry, later a manager and pitching coach, was catching Koufax in an Orlando, Florida, exhibition game in 1960 when he imparted some invaluable advice. After Koufax walked the first three batters using a curve and a change-up, he started throwing his fastball at full velocity. Sherry told Koufax to ease up on the fastball and let his fielders do the work. Koufax gave it a try and struck out the side. He pitched four more scoreless innings, walking only one, and began to realize what he could accomplish by not overthrowing. During the next six seasons, Koufax won three Cy Young Awards and five ERA titles, paving his path to Cooperstown.

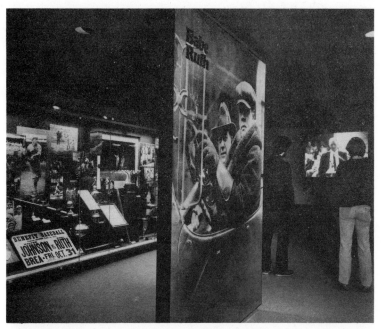

In the Babe Ruth Exhibit at the Baseball Hall of Fame and Museum, the dominant figure in American sports is recalled with a unique collection of memorabilia. A film on Babe is shown continuously. In the foreground, Babe is shown in his automobile with Yankee manager Miller Huggins.

68. Ed Walsh, 1.82, and Addie Joss, 1.88.

69. Dutch Leonard of the Red Sox had a 1.01 mark in 1914. Three-Finger Brown of the Cubs had a

1.04 mark in 1906, but Bob Gibson of the Cardinals is generally credited with the NL record, 1.12 in 1968, because ERA did not become an official statistic until 1912.

70. Eddie Mathews.

71. Nelson Fox.

72. Luke Appling of the White Sox, 1930–50.

73. Bob Feller of the Indians, 1936–56.

74. Pitcher, 46.

75. Third base, 7.

· 11 ·
TRADITIONS

Baseball is a game of tradition; it is slow to change. It is, in the words of the late club owner Bill Veeck, a game to be savored, not gulped.

When a change does occur in baseball, it is often implemented many years after it was first suggested.

Consider the designated-hitter rule, introduced by the American League in 1973. Although it was considered a radical innovation, the idea for the designated hitter had been on the back burner for some 45 years.

The seventh-inning stretch, spring training, uniform numbering, batting practice, and even the practice of chewing tobacco are time-honored baseball traditions. So are the assorted rituals associated with superstition, Edmund Burke's "religion of feeble minds."

Even the location of the Baseball Hall of Fame in Cooperstown is justifiable *by tradition*. The rural upstate New York hamlet is hard to reach by automobile or mass transportation, but it is the site of the game's most hallowed shrine because unsubstantiated legends suggest the sport was "invented" there.

As long ago as 1910, a president started the tradition of throwing out the first ball on Opening Day. The playing of the national anthem before every game began more than 30 years later.

"Days" for retiring heroes have been traditional since the tearful Yankee Stadium farewells of Lou Gehrig and Babe Ruth. A happier time is the six-week period of spring training, when athletes round into playing shape in an atmosphere so casual that autographs are more plentiful than hot dogs. Spring training certainly qualifies as a baseball tradition. It should: it features day games on the real grass of roofless ballparks.

• SCORING •

Do you rate as a strong baseball traditionalist? See for yourself:

27–30   Grade A. Wear white for purity—you know your stuff.

25–26   Grade B. Like Dick Allen, don't play on it if cows don't eat it.

22–24   Grade C. You're just above the Mario Mendoza Line of mediocrity.

20–21   Grade D. Your average has slipped into Mario Mendoza territory.

Under 20   Grade F. You can't hit your weight—try another sport.

• QUESTIONS •

1.   What number was Babe Ruth wearing when he hit his 60th home run?

2.   Why did Babe Ruth wear number 3?

3.   What Yankee wore number 3 after Babe Ruth and number 7 before Mickey Mantle?

4.   Name two players whose numbers were retired by two different clubs.

5.   What number did Honus Wagner wear?

6.   Who was Joe Earley?

7.   What radio station was the first to broadcast baseball?

8.   Who was the first batting-practice pitcher?

9.   How did the seventh-inning stretch originate?

10. What is the origin of Bat Day?

11. Who was the Clown Prince of Baseball?

12. How did the hot dog get its name from baseball?

13. Where did baseball get the idea of dragging the infield?

14. What is the hidden-ball trick?

15. Why is the national anthem played before games?

16. Did night baseball start in the minor leagues?

17. Why do the Yankees wear pinstripes?

18. Why do the Reds always open their season in Cincinnati?

19. What was the reserve clause?

20. Why did the majors twice resort to a split-season format?

21. How did spring training originate?

22. Why did teams hold spring training in the North for three years?

23. Who was the only person to play for the New York Rangers hockey team, the New York Knickerbockers basketball team, and the Brooklyn Dodgers?

24. The actor who played the title role in *The Babe Ruth Story* was once Ruth's batboy. Name him.

25. Which political figure kept baseball going during World War II?

26. Who caught a ball thrown from the top of the Washington Monument?

27. Who was Hilda Chester?

28. Who originated batting practice?

29. Why did Ralph Branca switch his number from 13 to 12?

30. What habits are believed to bring good luck in baseball?

• ANSWERS •

1. He was not wearing a number. The Yankees began wearing numbers two years later.

2. When the Yankees first assigned uniform numbers to their players, they issued them in the sequence of the batting order. Ruth batted third, so he got number 3. Lou Gehrig, batting behind him, was given number 4.

Newsreel versions of "Babe Ruth's 60th home run" are phony if the slugger's back bears his famous number. The Yankees wore no numbers during the season (1927) when Ruth hit 60.

3. Cliff Mapes, an outfielder who hit .242 in five seasons, reached the majors in 1948, before the Yankees had retired Ruth's number. When the team decided to honor the dying slugger on Babe Ruth Day that summer, the number was retired and Mapes had to pick a new uniform. He chose number 7, a number he relinquished before Mantle arrived in 1951.

4. Hank Aaron's number 44 was retired by the Atlanta Braves and Milwaukee Brewers; Casey Stengel's number 37 was retired by the Yankees and Mets.

Hank Aaron's number has been retired more than once.

5. Wagner, who played from 1897 to 1917, never wore a number as a player but later wore number 33 as a Pittsburgh coach. That number was officially retired by the Pirates in his honor.

6. Earley was the night watchman honored by the Indians' owner, Bill Veeck, after his letter to the *Cleveland Press* suggested that teams hold "days" for fans who needed the money instead of for well-paid stars who didn't. Earley got a series of gag gifts, including an outhouse and a backfiring Model T, before receiving a Ford convertible, a refrigerator, a washing machine, luggage, a watch, clothes, and cash. A crowd of 60,405 attended "Good Old Joe Earley Night" on September 28, 1948.

7. Pittsburgh's KDKA broadcast the first game, a Pirate-Phillie clash on August 5, 1921.

8. Paul Shreiber became the first batting-practice pitcher when the Yankees hired him in 1937. Before that, teams routinely used regular pitchers to throw batting practice.

9. There are different theories. One suggests that fans of the Cincinnati Red Stockings of 1869, the

first professional team, stood in the seventh inning to gain temporary relief from the hard wooden benches then in use. Another indicates that fans in Washington stood out of respect for the office of president when William Howard Taft appeared to be leaving in the seventh inning of the 1910 opener (he was merely stretching). Other historians believe that the seventh-inning stretch began in 1882, when Manhattan College coach Brother Jasper instructed his student spectators not to move about or leave their seats while a game was in progress. He relented in the seventh inning on an afternoon when the students seemed especially restless. The coach stopped the game and told the fans to stretch their legs—in the seventh inning.

10. In 1952 St. Louis Browns' business manager Rudie Schaeffer bought 12,000 bats from a supplier in a closeout sale. He then announced they would be given away at a doubleheader. More than 15,000 fans attended—a big crowd for the hapless Browns—and a new promotion was born. Other gimmicks, such as Cap Day, Photo Album Day, and Seat Cushion Night, were spawned by the success of Bat Day.

11. Al Schacht and Max Patkin both deserve the title. Schacht and Washington teammate Nick Altrock toured ballparks, mostly in the minors, with their comedy act billed as a pregame promotion. Patkin began his clowning career in 1951 and has traveled more than three million miles since. Patkin, known for his ability to twist his body into all kinds of odd positions, has performed in more than 4,000 ballparks.

12. Veteran ballpark vendor Harry M. Stevens, who created the first scorecard in Columbus, Ohio,

before the turn of the century, began to handle concessions for the New York Giants in 1894. Seven years later, ice cream wasn't selling on a cold spring day so Stevens sent out for sausages, boiled them, slipped them into rolls, and sent his hawkers through the stands yelling, "Get 'em while they're hot!" Cartoonist Tad Dorgan supplied the name "hot dog" to the Stevens sausages, which reminded him of dachshunds. It was also Stevens who came up with a portable way to keep hot dogs hot; his vendors paraded around the stands with frank-loaded hot-water tanks strapped to their necks.

13. Infield dragging began in the Pacific Coast League in 1949, when Hollywood Stars manager Fred Haney decided fans would buy more concessions if there were a 10-minute break in the middle of a game. Haney came up with the brainstorm—now universal in baseball—while pondering a suggestion from concessions chief Danny Goodman on how to hike business.

14. The hidden-ball trick occurs when an infielder tricks a runner into thinking the pitcher has the ball. Actually, the infielder has the ball, and the pitcher is merely cooperating with his teammate by pretending he has it.

15. Pregame playing of "The Star-Spangled Banner" began as a morale builder in 1942, the first full year of American involvement in World War II. It soon became a tradition.

16. Yes. The first night game in professional baseball occurred in 1930, when Independence, Kansas, of the Western Association lost to Muskogee, 13–3, under a primitive lighting system. Des Moines followed suit, and the team's fans were so taken with the "madness under moonlight"

that the team played another night game the next night. Team president E. Lee Keyser said night ball would be the salvation of the minors because it attracted families and working people who could not attend weekday daylight games. The same logic was applied to night games in the majors a few years later.

17. After the 1914 season, Yankee management decided it would outfit New York players with uniforms that reflected Wall Street's "dressed for success" look. When the team took the field on April 22, 1915, Yankee players sported dark, vertical pinstripes on their home white uniforms.

18. Because Cincinnati had the first professional team, the National League salutes that heritage by allowing the Reds to open at home every year. The Reds have done so every year they have been in the league (they were out from 1882 to 1889) except for 1877, when rain forced cancellation of the opener for three days. Tired of waiting for skies to clear, the Red Stockings boarded a boat for nearby Louisville, where they opened the season on a dry diamond.

19. The reserve clause, created at a National League meeting in Buffalo on September 29, 1879, bound a player to his club until it sold, traded, or released him. Though early players considered it an honor to be included among the five players each club could keep "in reserve" as protection from raids by rival teams, later players equated the reserve clause with slavery and said it retarded their career development. The reserve clause was effectively overturned after the 1975 season, when an arbitrator allowed Andy Messersmith and Dave McNally to become free agents. The pitchers had refused

to sign 1975 contracts containing the reserve clause.

20. Baseball used a "split season" format most recently in 1981. When a seven-week player strike interrupted the season, league executives, working in concert with the commissioner's office, declared that league leaders on June 12, when the strike began, would be considered first-half champions. Teams in first place from August 10 to season's end would be second-half champions. An extra week of playoffs—a best-of-five division series between the two half-season champions in each of the four divisions—was added to the regular postseason format. Though the 1981 split season was designed to regain fans turned off by the strike, it also created controversy when neither the Cardinals nor the Reds—the teams with the National League's best overall winning percentages for 1981—qualified for postseason play.

    A previous split season was tried in 1892, when the National League was the only major circuit in operation. The format, modeled after a successful Eastern League experiment in 1891, included a best-of-nine playoff between the two winners. Fan interest was limited, however, so the split season was abandoned after one year. Fan interest was rekindled the following year when an increase in the pitching distance—from 50 feet to today's 60 feet, 6 inches—produced games with greater offensive production.

21. A touring semipro club from Chicago, seeking to beat the undefeated Cincinnati Red Stockings, went to New Orleans for rigorous preseason training in 1870. The first spring training by a professional team was believed to be the work-

outs conducted by the National League's Chicago White Stockings, managed by Cap Anson, in Hot Springs, Arkansas, in 1886, 10 years after the NL was founded. Anson had been disgusted with the extra weight his players had added during the winter and wanted them to sweat it off.

22.   The "Landis Line," established by baseball commissioner Kenesaw Mountain Landis for the springs of 1943-44-45, kept big-league teams close to home during World War II. Landis, seeking to keep rail transportation open for the nation's war needs, ruled that no team could train south of the Ohio or Potomac rivers or west of the Mississippi (with the exception of the two St. Louis clubs). As a result, spring training datelines in 1943 came from such places as French Lick, Indiana (Cubs); College Park, Maryland (Senators); Bear Mountain, New York (Dodgers); Atlantic City, New Jersey (Yankees); and Wilmington, Delaware (Phillies).

23.   Organist Gladys Goodding.

24.   William Bendix.

25.   President Franklin D. Roosevelt sent a "green-light letter" to Commissioner Kenesaw Mountain Landis in which he urged that baseball continue, as a morale booster.

26.   William (Pop) Schriver, catcher for the Cubs, was the first, on August 25, 1894, but Gabby Street's 1908 catch from the same structure got more publicity because it was arranged by drama critic Pres Gibson, a friend of Street's, to settle a bet. With the wind a factor, Street caught only the last of the 13 balls dropped from the top of the 508-foot monument.

27. Hilda Chester, an enthusiastic fan of the Brooklyn Dodgers, was the head cheerleader of the Ebbets Field faithful during the 1940s. Known as the "Belle of Ebbets Field," she constantly rang a loud cowbell—after receiving medical advice that exercising her arm in the sun would help her rheumatism. The cowbell weighed four pounds.

28. Harry Wright, manager of the Phillies from 1884 to 1893, was the first to mandate batting practice. He required each player to hit 12 balls as part of a pregame exercise program. He also had fungo hitters hit fly balls to outfielders. Wright's routine attracted crowds who wanted to see their favorites hit—even if only during "practice." Modern batting practice can take anywhere up to two hours (for both teams), a routine longer than the pregame ritual of any other sport.

29. The number 13 was widely associated with bad luck even before Ralph Branca, pitching for the Brooklyn Dodgers, threw the pitch that turned a 4–2 ninth-inning lead into a 5–4 deficit in the final game of the 1951 Giant-Dodger playoff. Bobby Thomson hit the pitch into the left-field seats at the Polo Grounds on October 3, 1951. The following season, Branca wore number 12.

30. Ballplayers have always felt that good-luck rituals might help and can't hurt. Among "good luck charms" are knocking on wood; carrying a rabbit's foot, four-leaf clover, or other charm; swinging two bats in addition to the regular bat while loosening up; seeing empty barrels; putting on the left shoe first; having the pitcher get the ball from the same man each inning; finding a lucky hairpin that will inspire a slew of hits; stepping on third base or another base before

taking a fielding position; and wearing the same clothes, eating the same food, and doing the same things while on a hot streak.

Players say it is bad luck to chew gum instead of tobacco (many chew a mixture); walk between the catcher and umpire when coming to bat; step on the foul lines; put a hat on a hotel bed; open an umbrella in a room; see a black cat; or have anything to do with the number 13—on or off the field.

• 12 •
TRADES

Teams trade players—and even managers—more often than kids trade baseball cards.

Provisions of the Basic Agreement between players and management sometimes force clubs to secure permission from players before completing deals, but the ritual of constant dealing continues to be an integral part of the game.

During baseball's winter meetings, a weeklong December convention that brings together major- and minor-league officials, trades sometimes happen so frequently that fans have trouble keeping track.

No player is immune to the trade market. Such superstars as Babe Ruth, Rogers Hornsby, Jimmie Foxx, Hank Greenberg, Warren Spahn, and Hank Aaron experienced at least one trade each.

"Being traded is like celebrating your 100th birthday," says television commentator Joe Garagiola. "It might not be the happiest occasion in the world, but consider the alternatives."

"Trading is hoping," explains Maury Wills, who was sold or traded three times as a player. "General managers trade for what they hope will happen. There's never been a general manager who's so brilliant he can guarantee a sure-shot trade. Show me a general manager with a reputation as a shrewd trader and I'll show you a man who's been lucky."

Since 1976, movement of players has also resulted from free agency and the fall of the old reserve clause.

• SCORING •

Would you trade your mother-in-law for a player to be named later? If you're a trader who likes to gamble, you might. In life, as in baseball, you know what you have but you don't always know what you're getting. To determine how much you know about baseball trades, use this scoring system:

22-25	Grade A. You merit a no-trade clause in your contract.
20-21	Grade B. Frank Lane would be proud.
17-19	Grade C. You qualify for the figurehead job of general manager for George Steinbrenner.
15-16	Grade D. You're smarter than Charley Finley's mule.
Under 15	Grade F. Harry Frazee would swindle you in a straight swap.

• QUESTIONS •

1. The Indians and Tigers exchanged a home-run king for a batting king. Who were they?

2. The Indians and Tigers traded managers that same year. Who were the pilots?

3.   Name the Cleveland and Detroit front-office executives who were behind the trade of managers.

4.   Whom did the Braves get from the Brewers for Hank Aaron?

5.   The Orioles traded three players to the Reds for Frank Robinson. Name at least one of them.

6.   Name at least one pitcher traded midway through a 20-win season.

7.   Whom did the Mets send to the Giants for Willie Mays?

8.   How did the Yankees get Babe Ruth?

9.   Who was the first player selected in the reentry draft?

10. Whom did the Yankees get for Willie McGee?

The Yankees thought they were too deep in outfielders to keep Willie McGee down on the farm.

11. Whom did the Dodgers get when they sent pitcher Bruce Ellingsen to the Indians?

12. What brother battery was traded by the Red Sox?

13. Who broke the ice during baseball's initial interleague trading period in 1959?

14. How did Kirk Gibson become a Dodger?

15. What announcer was traded for a catcher?

16. Why did the Phillies trade a 30-game winner?

17. Why did the Phillies trade a Triple Crown winner?

18. After playing for the Braves in three cities, Hall of Famer Eddie Mathews was traded twice. Where?

19. Jackie Robinson retired rather than report to the team that acquired him in a trade. Identify the team.

20. Pitcher Ernie Broglio was sent from St. Louis to the Cubs in a deal involving a future Hall of Famer. Who was he?

21. After twin salary disputes, the Mets traded two top stars on the trading deadline of June 15, 1977. Who were they and where did they go?

22. Longtime Braves' star Warren Spahn split his final big-league season between two other NL clubs. Name them.

23. True or false? Hall of Famers Al Kaline, Brooks Robinson, Mickey Mantle, and Ernie Banks were never traded.

24. What catcher reversed his double-digit uniform number when he changed his Sox via free agency?

25. Name one of the two pitchers the Mets sent to St. Louis for Keith Hernandez.

Keith Hernandez was a National League MVP for the Cardinals before he was traded to the Mets.

• ANSWERS •

1. Home-run king Rocky Colavito went from Cleveland to Detroit for batting champion Harvey Kuenn on April 17, 1960.

2. Joe Gordon of the Indians went to Detroit for Jimmie Dykes on August 3, 1960.

3. Frank Lane of Cleveland and Bill DeWitt of Detroit.

4. Outfielder Dave May and pitcher Roger Alexander.

5. Milt Pappas, Jack Baldschun, and Dick Simpson.

6. Hank Borowy in 1945 and Rick Sutcliffe in 1984 completed 20-win seasons with the Cubs after starting those seasons elsewhere. Borowy came from the Yankees, Sutcliffe from the Indians.

7. Pitcher Charlie Williams.

8. Because Red Sox owner Harry Frazee needed funds to underwrite his theater productions, and because he was willing to sacrifice athletics for dramatics, he started selling stars after Boston's World Championship of 1918. With the Yankee office two doors from Frazee's New York headquarters, he had a short walk and an eager customer. By 1923, 11 of his stars were Yankees. Ruth, the biggest, was sold to New York for $125,000, then a staggering sum, on January 3, 1920.

9. Reggie Jackson. The Montreal Expos, drafting negotiating rights in the 1976 reentry draft, the first of its kind, made Jackson their first choice.

10. Pitcher Bob Sykes went from St. Louis to the Yankees on October 21, 1981. Sykes, a 26-year-old left-hander with a 23–26 career record, never won another big-league game. McGee, on the other hand, helped lead the Cardinals to the 1982 World Championship and was MVP and batting king when the Cardinals won the pennant three years later.

11. Pedro Guerrero. The deal for the unknown 17-year-old slugger occurred on April 3, 1974, five days before Hank Aaron hit his record-breaking 715th home run against the Dodgers.

12. Wes and Rick Ferrell were traded together by the Red Sox to the Senators on June 10, 1937, along with outfielder Mel Almada, for outfielder Ben Chapman and pitcher Bobo Newsom.

Pedro Guerrero was 17 when his contract was acquired in trade by the Los Angeles Dodgers.

13.   The Red Sox and Cubs made the first official swap of the interleague trading period. On the first day, November 21, 1959, the Sox sent first baseman Dick Gernert to the Cubs for pitcher Dave Hillman and first baseman-outfielder Jim Marshall.

14.   Given a second chance at free agency when arbitrator Tom Roberts gave a "second look" at seven premier free agents from the Class of 1985, Gibson opted to leave the Tigers and accept a lucrative offer from the Dodgers. Roberts, in making his ruling, had found that baseball club owners colluded to restrict the movement of veteran free agents.

15.   Ernie Harwell was broadcasting games for the Atlanta Crackers in 1948 when Dodger executive Branch Rickey, passing through town, happened to hear him. Rickey, needing an announcer to replace the ailing Red Barber, contacted Cracker owner Earl Mann to ask for Harwell's release. Mann agreed to release Harwell in exchange for the contract of Cliff Dapper, a catcher with the Brooklyn farm club in

Montreal. Harwell, now with the Tigers, has been in the major leagues since.

16. After going 30–13 for the 1917 Phillies, Grover Cleveland Alexander was drafted for World War I military service. Owner William Baker, uncertain his star would return intact, swapped him to the Cubs rather than take a chance. Alexander appeared only three times in 1918, but won 16 in 1919 and 27 in 1920. He returned to the Phillies for his final major-league season 10 years later.

17. Chuck Klein led the NL with a .368 batting average, 28 homers, and 120 RBI in 1933 but was traded by the Phillies to the Cubs on November 21, 1933, for pitcher Ted Kleinhans, infielder Mark Koenig, outfielder Harvey Hendrick, and $65,000. The Phils, hurting financially in the wake of the Great Depression, probably coveted the cash more than the players.

18. Houston and Detroit.

19. New York Giants.

20. Lou Brock.

21. Tom Seaver to Cincinnati and Dave Kingman to San Diego.

22. New York Mets and San Francisco Giants.

23. True.

24. Carlton Fisk went from 27 to 72 when he left the Red Sox for the White Sox after the 1980 season.

25. Neil Allen, Rick Ownbey.

• 13 •
TERMINOLOGY

Baseball's rich heritage is best expressed in its colorful language, most of which has found its way into everyday usage. Among the baseball terms now in popular use are *fan, ace, southpaw, rookie, double-header, rhubarb,* and *charley horse.*

If a salesman fails to close a deal, he has *struck out.* If a girl rejects a boy's advances, he can't get to *first base.* If a luncheon speaker can't keep his date, he asks for a *rain check* or, if that proves impractical, sends a *pinch hitter.* A competitor who loses out on a bid is *shut out.*

An entirely different language is used in the dug-outs, where players refer to *pull* or *spray* hitters, enjoy *taking a cut* at the plate but not at the salary table, and resent managers who use a *platoon* system or *go by the book.*

Many prominent quotations have stemmed from baseball personalities, both on the field and off. Branch Rickey earned his niche in the baseball quotebook by saying, "The trades you don't make are your best ones." The young Yogi Berra once confided, "Bill Dickey is learning me all his experiences." Not to be outdone, Ralph Kiner told a 1988 television audience, "Pascual Perez has won all eight of his victories."

Nicknames, an important aspect of baseball language, began after more than one team surfaced in the same city. Early newspaper reports referred to the New Yorks or Bostons, although the first nickname had been established with the 1845 creation of Alexander Cartwright's Knickerbocker Base Ball Club of New York.

Both team and player nicknames often come from the animal kingdom: Tigers, Blue Jays, Cardinals, Cubs, Hippo Vaughn, Rabbit Maranville, etc.

• SCORING •

Reading *Bartlett's Familiar Quotations* won't help you run up a big score in this chapter. But rudimentary knowledge of baseball history should help. Use the following guidelines:

45–50   Grade A. The Old Perfesser strikes again.

40–44   Grade B. First call from the bullpen.

35–39   Grade C. The fastball is fading.

30–34   Grade D. And you thought Casey was confused!

Under 30   Grade F. Never trust anyone under 30.

• QUESTIONS •

1.   Who said, "Don't look back, something may be gaining on you"?

2. Who said, "Nice guys finish last"?

3. Identify the player who said, "Home-run hitters drive Cadillacs, singles hitters drive Fords."

4. Who boasted that he "hit 'em where they ain't"?

5. What is Sparky Anderson's real first name?

6. What is Tom Seaver's real first name?

7. How did Home Run Baker get his nickname?

Frank (Home Run) Baker of the Philadelphia Athletics was a member of the famed "$100,000 Infield."

8. Why were the Waner brothers called Big Poison and Little Poison?

9. What was the name of Roy Hobbs's bat in *The Natural*?

10. Who was Aunt Minnie?

11. Why are spectators called fans?

12. What are "Chinese home runs"?

13. Why is a home run called a gopher ball?

14. What is a suicide squeeze?

15. Why is a left-hander called a southpaw?

16. What is a Texas Leaguer?

17. Why were the Cardinals once called the Gas House Gang?

18. What team was called the Hitless Wonders?

19. Why are the Yankees known as the Bronx Bombers?

20. What was the Big Red Machine?

21. Whose fans dubbed their team "Dem Bums"?

22. How did the Giants get their nickname?

23. How did George Herman Ruth get the name Babe?

24. Who was the Georgia Peach?

25. Identify the pitchers known as Big Six and The Big Train.

26. Why was Phil Regan called the Vulture?

27. Why was Hank Aaron called Bad Henry?

28. Why is a ballfield called a diamond?

29. What well-known manager said, "You can't win 'em all"?

30. What Hall of Fame pitcher said, "I'd rather be lucky than good"?

31. What slugger said, "You're a hero one day and a bum the next"?

32. Name two broadcasters who use the phrase "Holy Cow!"

33. Who was Dr. Strangeglove?

34. What is a banjo hitter?

35. How did the bullpen get its name?

36. Why is a team's top pitcher known as its ace?

37. Why is a first-year player called a rookie?

38. Who were the Yankee Clipper and the Splendid Splinter?

39. How did Yogi Berra get his nickname?

40. Why was Willie Mays known as the Say Hey Kid?

41. What star was told by a fan to "Say it ain't so, Joe"?

42. Who said, "It's not whether you win or lose but how you play the game"?

43. Why was Denton True Young better known as Cy?

Few fans know the real name of baseball's winningest pitcher: Denton True Young.

44. Why is a baseball fight called a rhubarb?

45. How did a Speaker of the House of Representatives acquire a baseball nickname?

46. Why was Charles Dillon Stengel known as Casey?

47. Who was the Wild Horse of the Osage?

48. What Hall of Famer was named for another?

49. How did Satchel Paige get his nickname?

50. Why is a leg injury often called a charley horse?

• ANSWERS •

1. Satchel Paige.

2. Leo Durocher, manager of the Brooklyn Dodgers in 1948, actually said "Nice guys finish eighth,"

when talking about rival Mel Ott of the New York Giants. Since the National League then had eight teams, writers interpreted the remark to mean, "Nice guys finish last." Ironically, the incorrect quote is the only baseball saying that appears in *Bartlett's Familiar Quotations.*

3. Ralph Kiner.

Fiery field boss Leo Durocher spent two-dozen years as a major-league manager but is best remembered for a distorted quote, delivered during his days as pilot of the Brooklyn Dodgers.

4. Wee Willie Keeler, one of five original Baltimore Orioles enshrined in the Baseball Hall of Fame, made the remark while boasting to a writer that he sent balls between fielders to get his hits. Keeler, an outstanding place hitter, compiled a 44-game hitting streak (later equaled by Pete Rose for the NL record) between April 22 and June 18, 1897.

5. George.

6. George.

7. Frank (Home Run) Baker earned his nickname by hitting crucial World Series home runs against Rube Marquard and Christy Mathewson, aces of

the New York Giants, in 1911. Baker's two-run homer off Marquard gave the Philadelphia Athletics a 3–1 victory in Game 2, while his ninth-inning shot off Mathewson the next day tied a game the Athletics eventually won, 3–2. Philadelphia went on to win the World Series in six games.

Ralph Kiner, now a broadcaster for the Mets, was known for his home-run bat as well as quotable quotes.

8. A Brooklyn fan, seeing them in action for the first time, noted that Paul Waner seemed to be a little heavier than brother Lloyd. He told them, in typical Brooklynese, "I see you're a big person and a little person!" Teammates overheard and the nicknames stuck. Statistically, Paul Waner was also "Big Poison." His career batting average was .333, 17 points higher than his brother's. Both men are members of the Hall of Fame.

9. Wonderboy.

10. Aunt Minnie was a fictitious character created by Pittsburgh play-by-play announcer Rosey Rowswell. When Ralph Kiner was cracking fre-

quent home runs for the Pirates in the late 1940s, Rowswell visualized a little old lady with an apartment window facing Forbes Field. When the ball seemed headed in her direction, he told listeners, "Open the window, Aunt Minnie, here it comes!" Then he smashed a light bulb near the microphone to produce the desired sound effect.

11. During the 1880s, German-born Chris Von der Ahe, owner of the St. Louis Browns of the American Association, was discussing a devoted St. Louis patron with sportswriter Sam Crane. "Dot feller is a regular FAN-a-tic," said the executive, emphasizing the first syllable of the last word in his accented English. Crane proceeded to put the abbreviated word into everyday usage.

12. Two New York sportswriters of the 1920s used the word *Chinese* to describe "unworthy" home runs. *New York Tribune* sports editor Bill McGeehan noted that the right-field wall of the Polo Grounds, home of the New York Giants, stood just 258 feet from home plate and looked as thick and formidable as the Great Wall of China. The *Journal's* T. A. Dorgan, who enjoyed deprecating Giant victories, had another analogy. He had come from San Francisco, home of America's largest Chinese community, where the Chinese were willing to work for low wages. To Dorgan, Chinese (cheap) labor and Chinese (cheap) home runs had something in common.

13. Lefty Gomez of the Yankees called home-run pitches "gopher balls" because they "go for" four bases. The term survives in current baseball lingo.

14. A suicide squeeze occurs when there are less than two out and a runner on third breaks for home as the pitch is delivered. The batter at-

tempts to bunt the ball so that the runner can score. A safety squeeze—used only to push across the tying or lead run late in a game—occurs when the runner breaks for home *after* the bunt.

15.   Before the turn of the century, when baseball was played only during the daytime, ballparks were laid out with the pitcher's mound east of home plate. That was done so that the sun, setting in the west, would not interfere with the batter's vision. A left-handed pitcher, as he prepared to face the batter, held the ball in the hand (or paw) that faced south.

16.   When Art Sunday joined Toledo of the International League from Houston of the Texas League in 1889, he began to collect a series of bloop hits—too far out for the infielders and too far in for the outfielders. Because of the league he had just left, his bloops were dubbed "Texas Leaguers."

17.   The Cardinals were known as the Gas House Gang during the early 1930s. Pitcher Dizzy Dean, lamenting the fifth-place standing of the team in June 1934, said, "We'd be in first place if we were in the other league." Pepper Martin retorted, "They wouldn't let us in. They'd say we were a lot of gas house ballplayers." Martin was comparing the dirty uniforms of the Cardinals, an aggresive team on the bases, with the overalls worn by gas station attendants.

New York sportswriter Frank Graham, the first to refer to the Cards as the Gas House Gang in print, compared the club's dirty livery with the wretched appearance of the populace in New York's rundown Gas House district. The name first appeared in 1934, when the Cardinals defeated Detroit to become world champions.

18. The 1906 Chicago White Sox, winners of the AL flag but producers of only six home runs. The following season, the Sox hit only three home runs as a team!

19. Because Yankee Stadium is located in the Bronx and because the team always seems to have sluggers in abundance, the Yankees have long been known as the Bronx Bombers. The club always seemed to have sluggers in the wings. Joe DiMaggio came up just as Lou Gehrig bowed out; Mickey Mantle succeeded DiMaggio; and Bill Dickey was succeeded by another Hall of Fame catcher, Yogi Berra.

20. In the 10-year span 1970–79, the Cincinnati Reds won four NL pennants and two division titles in the NL West—all but the 1979 title under Sparky Anderson. The team consisted of seasoned veterans who made the team run like a well-oiled machine. Since they wore uniforms highlighted in red, writers covering the club called it the Big Red Machine. Key players included Pete Rose, Joe Morgan, Johnny Bench, Tony Perez, George Foster, and Dave Concepcion. From 1970 to 1977, a Red was National League MVP every year except for 1971 and 1974. Seldom has a team dominated for a decade like the Big Red Machine.

21. The Brooklyn Dodgers, inept during the 1930s and often the source of frustration for their fans even during successful seasons in the 1940s and 1950s, inspired countless cries of "Dem Bums" at Ebbets Field. The designation became so ingrained that Willard Mullins, cartoonist for the *New York Daily News*, drew a front-page cartoon after Brooklyn won its only World Championship, in 1955. The cartoon, portraying an oversized,

smiling bum, ran under a bold black headline that screamed, "WHO'S A BUM?"

22. Originally known as the Green Stockings, later the Mutuals, the Giants acquired their present nickname in 1885, when manager Jim Mutrie jumped for joy after a big play. "My giants!" he cried. A sportswriter heard him and the name stuck.

23. George Herman Ruth, signed by Jack Dunn's International League Baltimore Orioles in 1914, had a round, cherubic face as a 19-year-old. The first time he suited up, a teammate said, "Look at Dunn's new babe!" Later that spring, after the joy-riding Ruth was nearly decapitated by a hotel elevator, he was reprimanded by Dunn. A teammate, feeling sorry for him, said, "You know, you're just a babe in the woods!"

24. Ty Cobb, a native Georgian.

25. Christy Mathewson, longtime star of the Giants, was called Big Six after a speedy fire truck of his era. Walter Johnson of the Senators was called The Big Train because his smoking fastball looked like a speeding train to enemy hitters.

26. In 1966 Phil Regan was a 29-year-old reliever who went 14–1 and had 21 saves and a 1.62 ERA in 65 games for the Los Angeles Dodgers. He seemed to get a win or a save every time he pitched. Tired of seeing Regan get credit for all the wins—often for working an inning or less—starter Claude Osteen pinned the "Vulture" tag on him. Other pitchers began to refer to a save as a "vulch."

27. Star Dodger pitchers Sandy Koufax and Don Drysdale called Hank Aaron "Bad Henry" because he was such a good hitter. Reverse nick-

names are common in baseball.

28.   Although Alexander Cartwright's 1845 design for a regulation field, with bases 90 feet apart, is actually a square, the field seems diamond-shaped from the catcher's perspective (a true diamond shape has two acute and two obtuse angles). Another theory on the origin of the term suggests that baseball borrowed the term from American urban planning of the nineteenth century. Towns were generally built around squares that featured public buildings. In the East, those squares were known as diamonds.

29.   Connie Mack, manager of the Philadelphia Athletics, said it after suffering through a 117-loss season in 1916.

30.   Lefty Gomez.

31.   Babe Ruth.

32.   Harry Caray and Phil Rizzuto.

33.   Dick Stuart, iron-gloved first baseman for the Pirates during the late 1950s and early 1960s, earned the nickname after the release of a movie called *Dr. Strangelove*.

34.   A banjo hitter is a player who gets base hits on balls that are not hit very well. Ray (Snooks) Dowd of the 1924 Jersey City club is believed to be the first to apply the banjo reference. He suggested that balls hit by banjo hitters make "plunk" sounds when they hit the bat.

35.   At the turn of the century, most American ballparks had a large outfield billboard for Bull Durham tobacco. The company popularized its name by offering $50 to any player who hit the bull with a batted ball. Pitchers warmed up under the sign, which was often located in fair territory deep in the outfield.

        Some baseball historians believe the bullpen

got its name from the log enclosures pioneers used to fend off Indian attacks, such as make-shift jails of Wild West days, or the enclosures used at bullfights, which contained benches. Pitchers rested on similar benches, so those areas became referred to as bullpens.

36. Asa Brainard pitched every game for the un-beaten Cincinnati Red Stockings of 1869. When-ever a pitcher of the period did exceptionally well, he was called an "asa." That was eventu-ally shortened to "ace."

37. In chess, the rook—buried in the corner of the board—is often the last piece used in a game. In the early part of the century, older players shunned newcomers, and first-year men were often the last to be approached by teammates. The term was first mentioned in print by the *Chi-cago Record-Herald* in 1913.

38. Joe DiMaggio and Ted Williams, respectively.

39. As a youth in St. Louis, Lawrence Peter Berra had a habit of sitting cross-legged while watching movies. He was doing just that when he and some friends went to see an Indian travelogue that featured a Hindu fakir. His friend Jack Ma-guire turned to Berra and said, "You know, you look just like that yogi. That's what I'm going to call you, Yogi Berra!"

40. When he first surfaced in the major leagues, Mays said little more than "Hey!" Sportswriter Barney Kremenko pinned the "Say Hey Kid" tag on the timid rookie.

41. Shoeless Joe Jackson, after the 1919 Black Sox scandal.

42. Sportswriter Grantland Rice.

43. Young was an innocent farm boy when he tried out for the Canton, Ohio, team late in the last

century. Hoping to impress the manager, he fired blazing fastballs past Canton hitters. Two of the pitches were missed by the catcher and splintered the wooden grandstand behind home plate. The batter said to the manager, "Sign that kid, boss. He did more damage to your grandstand than a cyclone." Denton True was called "Cyclone" for a while before the nickname was shortened to "Cy."

44. The term "rhubarb" was first used to describe a baseball brawl in 1938, when Garry Schumacher of the *New York Journal–American*, writing about a Giant-Dodger battle, explained that winners of fights in Brooklyn usually forced losers to swallow bad-tasting rhubarb tonic.

45. Tip O'Neill, former U.S. Speaker of the House, got his nickname from James O'Neill, the 1887 batting champion. O'Neill hit .492 (walks counted as hits that year) and specialized in fouling off pitched balls to make pitchers work harder. Because of the volume of foul tips, St. Louis teammates started calling him "Tip." The name caught on among fans—especially in the Irish-American community, where he was a hero. Among those who named their sons after him was Thomas P. O'Neill of Massachusetts, whose son later became Speaker of the House.

46. Longtime manager Casey Stengel used to sign his name "Charles Stengel, K.C." because he hailed from Kansas City. Spotting that designation on his luggage, players picked up the "K.C." and dropped the "Charles." Other historians insist Stengel got his nickname from the poem "Casey at the Bat" because the title character struck out at the end. Stengel fanned frequently early in his career.

47. Pepper Martin's heroics in the 1931 World Series for St. Louis inspired the nickname. Martin ran the bases with abandon and played a swift, aggressive center field. Since he came from Oklahoma, home of the Osage Indian tribe, a St. Louis newsman began referring to him as the "Wild Horse of the Osage."

48. Mickey Mantle was named after Mickey Cochrane, though the latter's real name was Gordon Stanley Cochrane. Mantle's father, a Cochrane fan, named his son for the former Tiger standout. Cochrane acquired his nickname when he played for the Dover minor-league team in the Eastern Shore League. His manager there decided he looked Irish so he started calling him Mickey.

49. LeRoy Paige picked up his famous nickname as a youth when he earned extra money by carrying luggage at the Mobile, Alabama, train station.

50. The 1886 Chicago White Stockings, rained out of a game, found a dry racetrack seven miles away, got a tip from a teammate on a horse named Charley, and placed their bets on him. The horse not only broke last but stayed last and finished last. The next day, when a Chicago player pulled up lame, a quick-witted colleague called him "Charley horse."

   A few years later, another horse named Charley, overworked from pulling a cab in preautomobile days, was used to drag the infield for Sioux City of the Western League. The aged, tired animal moved with difficulty and seemed to have arthritis. It wasn't long before players began referring to any limp or leg injury as a "charley horse."

• 14 •
STATISTICS

Baseball's individual records are determined through the daily box scores. Keeping score is easy, but there is a variety of methods. In any system, the objective is to keep a complete and accurate record that can be read weeks—or years—later.

Scorecards come in two styles—with blank squares or with smaller squares within the squares. Fans prefer the first (and ballpark scorecards are made that way) because there's more room to write.

To guarantee uniformity in professional scoring, the *Official Playing Rules* of baseball includes a section on scoring regulations. Under any system, it is essential to keep track of substitutes, position changes, and all batting and pitching statistics. The "streamlined" box score adopted by the major wire services during the early 1970s dropped the practice of showing position changes, thereby making it impossible for the avid fan to follow the game as closely as he would like. *The Sporting News* became the sole source of boxes showing defensive movement of players.

Modern records are "unofficial" in many cases because statistics currently used in the game were not always recognized.

For example, the *Chicago Tribune* began reporting runs batted in during the 1880 season, but the idea received such a cool reception that it was discontinued until 1891, when the National League and American Association ordered their scorekeepers to keep track of RBI. By June, NL scorekeepers had abandoned the practice, and the AA folded after the season.

"Official" recognition of RBI came about in 1920. Won-lost records weren't kept until 1887; complete games in 1909; ERA in 1912; and saves in 1969. "Modern" records are considered those of the twentieth century.

• SCORING •

Some people are good with figures but lousy with numbers. If you're one of those, you might not want to score this chapter. Otherwise, be my guest:

17–20	Grade A. Go to the head of the math class.
15–16	Grade B. Skilled enough to be a players' agent.
13–14	Grade C. You're average in the game of averages.
11–12	Grade D. Time is passing; are you?
Under 11	Grade F. What the hell is a circumcised triangle?

• QUESTIONS •

1. How many innings must a pitcher work to qualify for the ERA title?

2. How does a relief pitcher qualify for a save?

3. How is a "magic number" determined?

4. Describe a situation in which a team made a triple play without the ball being hit.

5. How can a pitcher pitch a complete game without getting a decision?

6. What is a 6-4-3?

7. How can a pitcher strike out more than three hitters in an inning?

8. In figuring the standings, how are "games behind" determined?

9. How is batting average calculated?

10. How is slugging average calculated?

11. How is earned-run average calculated?

12. Why is the ERA the best gauge of a pitcher's prowess?

13. How is fielding average calculated?

14. How is won-lost percentage calculated?

15. Who is designated Number 1 in the scoring of a game?

16. What number represents the designated hitter in the lineup?

17. In scoring, what symbol is used to signify a home run?

18. Did baseball keep won-lost records for pitchers in its early years?

19. Before going to the current system of four balls and three strikes for each batter, a different ratio was used. What was it?

20. How is a box score "proved"?

• ANSWERS •

1. Under the current format, a pitcher must work 162 innings, or one for each game his team plays.

2. A pitcher earns a save when he is the finishing pitcher in a game won by his club but is not the winning pitcher, and if he meets one of the following conditions: (a) he enters the game with a lead of no more than three runs and pitches for at least one inning; (b) he enters the game, regardless of the count, with the potential tying run on base, at bat, or on deck; or (c) he pitches effectively for at least three innings.

3. Compute the number of games yet to be played, add one, then subtract the number of games ahead of the closest opponent in the loss column of the standings.

4. It is possible. For example, on Opening Day 1978 in Cincinnati, the Reds had Joe Morgan at second and George Foster at first. Houston pitcher Joe Sambito fanned Dan Driessen. Foster, breaking for second on the hit-and-run play, was caught in a rundown. Morgan was leaning to-

ward home, so shortstop Roger Metzger threw the ball to third baseman Enos Cabell, who tagged Morgan for the second out. Foster had headed back to first but then decided to try for second. Cabell fired to Metzger, who tagged Foster for the third out.

5.   Pitchers who are not relieved when an official game is forfeited get credit for a complete game but not for a win or loss. This freakish situation happened to Hall of Famer Warren Spahn in 1942.

6.   A shortstop-to-second-to-first double play.

7.   A catcher must hold the ball on strike three. If he doesn't, the batter can run to first base. If he reaches the bag safely before the ball is thrown to the first baseman, he can take the base. Numerous major-league pitchers—especially those throwing knuckleballs and other hard-to-catch pitches—have fanned four men in one inning. Joe Niekro, a knuckleballer working in a spring exhibition game for the Astros, once fanned five. His catcher, not surprisingly, was the iron-gloved Cliff Johnson, later deployed as a designated hitter in the American League.

8.   Games behind are determined by comparing the leading team's record with the trailing team's on a minus-plus basis. For instance, 12 victories and 4 losses, against 7 victories and 8 losses, is a difference of 5 victories and 4 losses. The total of nine is then divided by two, indicating a difference of 4-1/2 games.

9.   Divide the number of hits by the number of at-bats.

10.   Divide the total bases of all safe hits by the number of at-bats.

11. Multiply the number of earned runs by nine (innings in a regulation game), then divide the result by the number of innings pitched.

12. Quality pitchers employed by inferior teams may lose more games than they win because of shabby offensive or defensive support. That is why earned-run average is a good gauge in determining the success of a pitcher. The ERA reflects the number of runs per game "earned" by opponents rather than yielded by inept defenders.

13. Divide the total putouts and assists by the total of putouts, assists, and errors.

14. Divide the number of victories by the total of games won and lost.

15. The pitcher.

16. None. Use the letters "DH" when a game is played with a designated hitter.

17. Four horizontal lines.

18. Not until 1887, when pioneer baseball writer Henry Chadwick began to record such statistics.

19. Five balls and four strikes was the ratio used briefly before 1889.

20. A box score is in balance, or proved, when the total of the team's times at bat, bases on balls, hit batters, sacrifice bunts, sacrifice flies, and batters awarded first base because of interference or obstruction equals the total of the team's runs, players left on base, and the opposing team's putouts.

· 15 ·
THEY ALSO PLAYED

Professional baseball includes not only the major leagues but also a complex network of minor-league teams, baseball in other countries, and—in the past—organized leagues that challenged the majors or gave those excluded from the majors a chance to play.

Minor-league baseball, the traditional training ground for the majors, gives talented players the chance to polish their skills and garner valuable experience that will eventually enable them to compete against the best ballplayers in the world.

Almost all major leaguers spend time in the minors, though Sandy Koufax, Al Kaline, and Catfish Hunter were notable exceptions. Ty Cobb, Rogers Hornsby, Babe Ruth, and Hank Aaron are among the game's immortals who began their pro baseball careers in the minors.

Except during the war years and the Great Depression, professional baseball has thrived throughout the century. But it probably would have done better if it had taken in the top stars of the Negro Leagues, two six-club circuits comprising baseball's best black talent. With blacks barred from the big leagues by an unwritten agreement among the owners, Negro League clubs provided outlets for many top players. A few—such as Satchel Paige, Monte Irvin, and Roy Campanella—eventually reached the majors, but most of those who did had spent their prime years playing in obscurity.

Modern Japanese teams would have much more difficulty beating major-league opponents than the old Negro League teams would have had. As in the United States, baseball is considered the national pastime of Japan.

Baseball outside the majors remains an integral part of the game's heritage. Avid fans should find the questions that follow enlightening.

• SCORING •

Could the Pittsburgh Crawfords, the greatest of the Negro League teams, have played in the majors? Was Josh Gibson better than Roy Campanella? Those questions will remain unanswered, but real experts will have solved the ones in this chapter. Rate yourself as follows:

17–20	Grade A. Prize: season tickets for the Denver Zephyrs.
15–16	Grade B. Major-league knowledge of minor-league subjects.
13–14	Grade C. A little more seasoning would be just right.
11–12	Grade D. Napoleon had Waterloo, Nixon had Watergate.
Below 11	Grade F. Marooned in the minors forever.

• QUESTIONS •

1. How many home runs did Babe Ruth hit in the minors?

2. What future Yankee star was the first man to have a 60-homer season in pro ball?

3. Name the only player to have two 60-homer seasons in pro ball.

4. Joe Bauman hit the most homers in a pro season. How many did he hit?

5. In 1981 Pawtucket and Rochester of the International League made history with a single game. What did they do?

6. What is the record for home runs in a professional game?

7. Who had the longest pro-ball hitting streak?

8. Who was the Japanese Babe Ruth?

9. Who was the Puerto Rican Babe Ruth?

10. Who was the black Babe Ruth?

Before Jackie Robinson integrated the majors, black players were restricted to the Negro Leagues.

11. Why are minor-league clubs known as farm teams?

12. What was the Federal League?

13. What was the Players League?

14. What was the Continental League?

15. What was "barnstorming"?

16. What league's all-star game was known as the East-West Game?

17. Who called his players "jumping beans" after they left for the Mexican League in 1946?

18. Who hit three homers in an inning during a minor-league game?

19. Of this team's 17 players, 16 made the majors—nine of them with the 1938 Yankees. Identify this minor-league powerhouse.

20. Joe DiMaggio hit in a record 56 major-league games but had an even longer hitting streak in the minors. How long was it?

• ANSWERS •

1. One, for Providence of the International League, at Toronto, on September 5, 1914. Ruth played in 46 minor-league games.

2. Tony Lazzeri had 60 homers and 222 RBI in 197 games for Salt Lake City in 1925.

3. Joe Hauser hit 63 for the 1930 Baltimore Orioles and 69 for Minneapolis of the American Associa-

tion three years later. His major-league total was 79 for six seasons.

4. Joe Bauman, 32, hit 72 home runs for the Roswell Rockets of the Class C Longhorn League in 1954. He never made it to the big leagues.

5. They played a 33-inning game. Pawtucket won, 3–2, in a game that started on April 18 and ended on June 23.

6. Nig Clarke of Corsicana had eight home runs in eight at-bats as his team crushed Texarkana, 51–3, at Ennis, Texas, on June 15, 1902. Corsicana players hit 21 home runs in the game, played in a nonleague park because of restrictions on Sunday baseball. Two other players went 8 for 8 in the game.

7. Joe Wilhoit hit in 69 straight games for Wichita in 1919.

8. Sadaharu Oh, a 6-foot, 174-pound slugger, helped the Tokyo Giants win nine straight pennants, 1965–73. He was a left-handed-hitting first baseman who became the "world" home-

Sadaharu Oh holds the "world" record for home runs.

run champion when he hit his 756th home run in 1977. He had run his total up to 868 by the time he retired.

9. Orlando Cepeda, star first baseman for the Giants, Cardinals, and Braves, was called the "Baby Bull" after his father, the "Bull," also known as the "Babe Ruth of Puerto Rico."

10. Josh Gibson was a power-hitting catcher who had several 70-homer seasons in the Negro Leagues before major-league baseball was integrated. In 1930, his first season, the 19-year-old Gibson slammed the only fair ball ever hit out of Yankee Stadium. He was chosen for the Negro League All-Star Game every year from 1933 to 1945, except for 1941, when he played in Mexico. Gibson hit .457 in 1936 and .440 in 1938—even though such pitches as the spitball, emery ball, mud ball, and shine ball (all banned in the majors) were legal in the Negro Leagues.

11. The farm-team concept came into usage at a time when some minor-league clubs operated as independents while others affiliated themselves with "parent" major-league organizations. The independents subsisted by selling or trading players to the majors, while the subsidized farm teams provided a place where big-league clubs could "grow their own" athletes and "harvest the crop."

12. The Federal League tried for two seasons, 1914–15, to establish itself as a third "major" league. It did attract several name players but was forced to rely chiefly on second-line talent and top minor leaguers. Lawsuits, failing finances, and the untimely death of powerful Brooklyn Federal League owner Robert Ward caused the circuit to collapse. A negotiated

peace was struck among the Federal League, National League, and American League on December 22, 1915.

13. When team owners announced a salary ceiling of $2,500 and strengthened the reserve clause before the 1890 season, many major leaguers revolted. Led by John Montgomery Ward, they found financial backing and ballparks for their new Players League. It provided such stiff competition that the American Association, then a major league, went under, and the National League was severely damaged. Exasperated owners, led by Al Spalding, bought out the Players League backers after the 1890 campaign and forced the players back into the NL, which expanded to 12 teams to absorb all the talent (it returned to its eight-club format by the turn of the century).

14. The Continental League was Branch Rickey's attempt to form a third major league in 1960. It collapsed in the planning stages when the American and National leagues agreed to expand to a number of cities that had been targeted for Continental League teams.

15. Before the advent of television, baseball enthusiasts who lived far from major-league cities got to see the stars play only through the postseason ritual of barnstorming. Both major leaguers and Negro League stars regarded barnstorming as an economic necessity, even though games were often played under dim lights in county-fair ballparks. Games were often played in small farm communities dotted with barns—accounting for the term "barnstorming."

16. Negro League.

17. Mel Ott, manager of the New York Giants, made the remark after Sal Maglie and other major leaguers jumped to the Mexican League in 1946, after Jorge Pasquel and four brothers offered lucrative contracts. Commissioner of Baseball A. B. (Happy) Chandler threatened the jumpers with five-year suspensions from organized ball, but a number of them went anyway. Most lasted only a year or two in Mexico before seeking to return.

18. Gene Rye, on August 6, 1930.

19. The 1937 Newark Bears.

20. While with the San Francisco Seals, DiMaggio hit in 61 consecutive games.

• 16 •
TODAY'S GAME

Baseball in the late 1980s is played by 26 teams, divided between two major leagues, which play 162-game schedules to determine divisional champions. Leaders of East and West in each league meet in a best-of-seven Championship Series to determine World Series opponents. Another best-of-seven set determines the world champion.

Because of the free-agent revolution that began in 1976, competitive balance in baseball has become a reality for most clubs. Each of the 12 National League clubs has won at least one divisional title since the new format was adopted in 1969; only a handful of American League entries have not. From 1978 to 1987, there were 10 different world champions in as many seasons.

Players have made handsome profits from free agency; more than 40 earn more than $1 million a season, and several—including Mike Schmidt, Dale Murphy, Don Mattingly, and Ozzie Smith—have reached the $2 million level.

The game has become a science as well as a sport. There are long and short relief pitchers, platoon players at key positions, and numerous specialists for pinch hitting, designated-hitter duties, and defensive substitution.

Controversy continues—both inside certain clubhouses and within the game's hierarchy. Only one of the two leagues uses the designated hitter, pitchers continuing to bat in the other (the DH league also has more teams than the older circuit); too many night games—especially at All-Star Game and World Series time—have alienated youngsters who would be the fans of tomorrow; and TV coverage, All-Star voting, and ballpark rowdyism too often detract from the fun of the game. But legions of devoted fans, with unswerving love of the game, set new attendance records every year.

• SCORING •

Fans of all ages keep close tabs on their heroes through newspapers, magazines, and radio-TV reports, as well as the burgeoning market in baseball cards and memorabilia. Since their knowledge of today's game is often comprehensive, this chapter was deliberately kept to a minimum. Use this chart to score:

13–15	Grade A. You know your baseball.
10–12	Grade B. Bridesmaid again.
8–9	Grade C. Too much time at the hot dog stand.
6–7	Grade D. Too casual, not enough fan.
Under 6	Grade F. Beer spills on your head from the upper deck.

• QUESTIONS •

1. In 1987 he fell one home run shy of becoming the second player to hit 40 home runs and steal 30 bases in the same year. Who was he?

2. This 1987 Cy Young Award winner and the man he was traded for two years previously both appeared in the Oakland All-Star Game. Name them.

3. Name the only rookie selected to play in the 1988 All-Star Game.

4. This team produced consecutive Rookies of the Year in 1986 and 1987.

5. What former Cy Young Award winner was sidelined with shoulder trouble for the entire 1987 season?

6. What former NL star returned from Japan to sign with a new major-league club for 1988?

7. Name the first man since Jim Palmer to win consecutive American League Cy Young Awards.

8. Name the only active NL player who has been both Rookie of the Year and Most Valuable Player (HINT: he did it in different seasons).

9. Identify the only active manager who had a 40-homer season in the majors.

10. Name the only active manager who won a batting title.

11. Who won the most games in the majors over the first half of the 1988 season?

12. What 1987 World Series opponents were traded for each other in 1988?

13. Name one of the two pitchers acquired by the Chicago Cubs for reliever Lee Smith.

14. What star left-hander answers to the nickname "Sweet Music"?

15. Who went into seventh place on the career home run list in 1988?

• ANSWERS •

1. Darryl Strawberry of the Mets.

Darryl Strawberry has made headlines not only for his play on the field but for his clubhouse comments about his teammates.

2. Steve Bedrosian of the Phillies and Ozzie Virgil of the Braves.

3. Chris Sabo of the Reds.

4. Oakland Athletics (Jose Canseco and Mark McGwire).

5. Bruce Sutter.

6. Bob Horner, formerly with the Braves, signed with St. Louis.

7. Roger Clemens of the Red Sox.

8. Andre Dawson

9. Dave Johnson of the Mets.

10. Pete Rose of the Reds.

11. Greg Maddux of the Cubs was 15-3 at the All-Star break.

12. Tom Brunansky of the Twins was traded to St. Louis for Tom Herr.

13. Calvin Schiraldi and Al Nipper were acquired from the Boston Red Sox.

14. Frank Viola of the Minnesota Twins.

15. Mike Schmidt passed Mickey Mantle to move into seventh place on the career home run list.